Mercury Rising

The inside story of Café Josie,
magic theme diner at the end of
the MADchester Universe

Josie Adamson

Additional research and sub-editing
by Richard Adamson

Copyright © 2020 Josie Adamson
All rights reserved.
ISBN:

DEDICATION

This memoir is dedicated to the eternal memory of Ivor Parry (1919-1996), news printroom overseer, Archdruid of Wales and close-up magician extraordinaire renowned throughout the world as Rovi.

There is, I believe, in many men, specially single men, a passion of dining out – a dinner engagement is so high in the class of their pleasures, their employments, their dignities, alms their duties, that anything gives way to it . . . he cannot refuse an invitation, he must dine out wherever he is asked.

JANE AUSTEN'S *EMMA*

CONTENTS

	Foreword Richard Adamson	1
	Prologue: Night Crawler & other grey spectres	5
1	The Vanishing	13
2	Total Recall	23
3	Transfixing Da Vinci	29
4	Plate Tectonics	39
5	Strip Chef Naked	51
6	Café Confidential	59
7	Mercury Rising	69
8	Zen, Balducci & the Force	83
9	Demons at Halloween	101
10	NeoRomantica Magicana	115
11	Legends of Legerdemain	137
12	Kitchen Impossible	149
13	Paradise Lost, the Final Days	161
	Pastscript: Back to the Future	177
	Appendix: Secrets for Sale	183

The work is rather too bright and sparkling; it wants to be stretched out here and there with a longer chapter – of sense if it could be had; if not, of solemn, specious nonsense about something unconnected with the story... a critique of Sir Walter Scott, a history of Bonaparte, or anything that would form a contrast, and bring the reader with increased delight to the playfulness and epigrammatism of the general style.

JANE AUSTEN'S ADVICE TO
HER ASPIRING NOVELIST NIECE ANNA

FOREWORD

I WAS AN EARLY RUNAWAY long before it was made fashionable in popular song (Del Shannon, 1961). The Sixties had exploded on to the world eight miles high over the frozen wastes of Sverdlovsk in the Urals, when a giant black bat was blasted out of the sky by Red rocketry. America's U2 spy plane had been overflying the Soviet Union for at least half a decade, to a chorus of White House denials.

But when shot-down U2 pilot Gary Powers was paraded before the world's press, the Russians thundered angry warnings to the West. Within months, work was started on building the Berlin wall. And at one fraught session of the United Nations, Communist leader Nikita Khrushchev took off his shoe to bang the podium and promised to bury Western imperialism. (But Nikita Sergeyevich had little to say about a spot of cultural imperialism, when British trad jazzman Kenny Ball purloined a popular Russian folksong, to score a transatlantic hit with *Midnight in Moscow*).

But notwithstanding all this feverish, political kerfuffle, this runaway aged two did attempt to make good my escape but was hauled back by my Aunty Flo who saved me from being run over by a passing Brit Army meat wagon in a New Delhi street (dear, sweet Aunty Flo long since departed to that Palace of Varieties in the sky).

Fast forward five years and I join our boys occupying (West) Germany just in time to catch a falling star. Or should I say, several stars. They were among more than half a dozen thumbnail sketches in my Mum's Christmas present *The Boys Book of Magic* – Jean Robert-Houdin, David Devant, John Nevil Maskelyne, Chung Ling Soo, Horace Goldin, Houdini. I got to know them all, all names to conjure with.

We were stationed in Hannover with the British Army of the Rhine. And I vaguely recall hearing on the radio (my Mum always had the BBC on) that the French Foreign Legion had been defeated at Dien Bien Phu. It made me wonder what chance we had of avoiding a similar fate, given we were so deep in enemy territory.

Then Satan came a'calling. The six-month-old, coal-black Labrador retriever was rescued and brought home from the Officers Mess by our Dad. But as he bounded into our house all huge paddle paws and floppy chops and was introduced, our Mum had a fit. We can't have a dog called after the Devil incarnate, she cried! A quick renaming ceremony took place, and Satan became Blackie – Schwarzer – auf Deutsch, and he was to be our faithful companion for many, many years.

Two years later, it was off to the theatre, the magnificent Stadthalle Opera House to see Kalanag perform all manner of illusions. He poured any drink requested from a huge copper kettle – just like Austria's Wolfgang Moser did on Penn and Teller in 2019. And tipped out a never-ending stream of water from a single Lota jug. And he made his exotic assistant Gloria float into mid-air and disappear. (Ach so, Asrah!). And a car with four people aboard also vanished from a brightly lit stage right before our very eyes. Poof! Sim-sala-bim! Then we too were gone, off back home from Germany, safe and sound.

Fast forward to the end of the decade and two Christmas conjuring sets later. Al Koran, a suave, former hairdresser, wows TV viewers with mind-reading feats that defied explanation. Then Johnny Hart goes one better with fast hands and a mesmerising smile. Suddenly, I wanted to learn how to pull card fans out of thin air and flocks of Java doves from inside my coat tails. No chance! Then playing football in the Welsh League and a career in journalism intervened. Twenty years later I had a dream and woke up to find I'd booked a table at a new theme diner called Café Josie.

It's been helluva ride on a long and winding road, a lifetime's journey that ended up right here. I wouldn't have missed it for the world. And neither should you.

RICHARD ADAMSON,
LINZ, UPPER AUSTRIA, JULY 2020

Gatecrashing the world famous Magic Circle

THE MAGIC CIRCULAR

DECEMBER 1987

Pictured here is Rovi, the Wizard of Wales caught in the act in a mirrored corner of Manchester's newest upmarket theme restaurant, Cafe Josie in the city's southern suburb of Chorlton

With him is restaurant co-owner and Manchester magician Richard Adamson whose declared aim in opening Cafe Josie is to put close-up restaurant table magic really on the map in Britain.

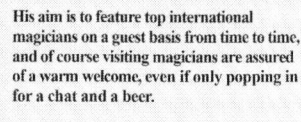

His aim is to feature top international magicians on a guest basis from time to time, and of course visiting magicians are assured of a warm welcome, even if only popping in for a chat and a beer.

This applies particularly to our colonial cousins from across the water who may be passing through via Manchester's international airport. Ringway is literally only 15 mins by taxi from the restaurant.

One Manchester close-upper who is rapidly making a a name for himself at Josie's tables is Order of Merit award-winner Dave Allen who has a regular Saturday night spot at the restaurant.

Magicians visiting Manchester are cordially invited to give Richie Adamson a ring on 061 861 0334.

☆   ☆   ☆   ☆

PROLOGUE:
NIGHT CRAWLER & OTHER GREY SPECTRES

*Oh judgment thou hath fled to
brutish beasts, and men have lost
their reason.*

MARK ANTHONY'S GRAVESIDE ORATION FOR

JULIUS CAESAR

OK. SO, YOU'RE READING these first few lines thinking wtf! Let me put you out of your misery. Suppose someone pointed a loaded gun at your head and demanded you reveal your wildest dream, and/or your worst nightmare. What would your life-saving answer be?

Well, with a finger on the trigger, you may well confess that it's to one day open a nice little restaurant in your neck of the woods, and then to live happily ever after. In your dreams, baby! Much more certain is that you'll fail spectacularly, like most who've tried to run with this fantasy.

But congratulations! Welcome to the party, you're not alone. There are tens of thousands, possibly millions, of us in here, all picking over the entrails of an absurdist dream and we're gonna have some fun. But a word or warning. If you quit now and stop reading, you're gonna die wondering!

Spoiler Alert!
Whoah! So, you've trolled down to here to what we in the business call the paradox paragraph (as in, who the hell ever reads it), and you're still thinking WTF! Time to reveal the Big Idea, the premise on which this whole box of frogs is based. Are you ready for this?

There's a symmetry, a synergy between cooking and conjuring which doth shape their ends, rough hew them how we will. But that's enough of the Bard transfixed. Back to simple English. It's no secret that the housewife, the woman in any partnership today, is the mistress of all she surveys in the kitchen. And that over the years, day after day, she concocts feasts fit for a king – and certainly far more tasty than the menu on offer at that new eatery that's just opened down the road.

Sounds a familiar idea? Yeah, of course. But what about the other half of this domestic equation, the male of the species? Well, ok, sometimes just occasionally, he too is no slouch in the rustling up grub stakes. Very occasionally. But for the most part, boys are not brought up learning the kitchen protocol of how to cook. They have to make do with a conjuring set, usually around the age of nine, at Christmas. And they drive everyone nuts for days, weeks, even years thereafter with their little box of miracles.

This obsession usually wears off around 16 or 17 when they discover that what skirts hide is much more interesting. And like those skirts, this story has been a long time swirling into reality. But even then, it might not have seen the light of day had not its principal inspirer decided to exit stage left without a bye or your leave in 2018. The sudden death of Anthony Bourdain, notorious chronicler of restaurant kitchen mafiosi, was the trigger for putting pen to paper, and which galvanised the telling of this tale.

Oh, and by the way, Bourdain had absolutely no doubt about boys! "I do think basic cooking skills are a virtue, the ability to feed yourself and others with proficiency, a fundamental skill. It should be taught to every young man and woman, and become as vital to growing up as learning how to wipe your own ass or cross the street by yourself."

As he was in life, so he was in death. One cannot scan the sheer eclecticism of Anthony Bourdain's literary and TV output not to come to the conclusion that he was totally aware he'd missed out on his life's true vocation – to be a storyteller and TV star. And he never stopped. Really! He presented no fewer than four wildly popular series on American TV – *A Cook's Tour*, *No Reservations*, *The Layover*, and *Parts Unknown*. And all while regularly filing eating out copy to, among others, *The Times*, *Observer*, *New York Times*, *New Yorker* and *Food Arts magazine*.

And Bourdain still had the time to pen a culinary cannon that included *Kitchen Confidential*, *Typhoid Mary*, *Les Halles Cookbook*, *No Reservations*, and *Medium Raw*. And he wrote fiction as well, with resplendent titles like *Bone in the Throat*, *Gone Bamboo*, *The Bobby Gold Stories*, *Get Jiro!*, and *Get Jiro: Blood & Sushi*.

Perhaps at the heart of the matter was Bourdain's realisation that he was running out of Wisdom's pearls to cast before the swinish multitude. He'd done it all, once, twice, three times – never like a lady! All that was left was darkness visible. And his response was to rage against the dying of the light. It's what we'd all do in similar circumstances. Perhaps. And if this doesn't strike a chord with you, or makes no sense at all, tread softly in view of what follows.

Extreme feelings of déjà vu would have engulfed us if the celebrity chef had been around at the time Café Josie was materialising as a spectral beast in our mind's eye. Bourdain's seminal book *Kitchen Confidential: Adventures in the Culinary Underbelly* would have been out (published 2000) as would a sequel *Medium Raw: A Bloody Valentine to the World of Food and the People who Cook* (published 2010).

Bourdain might have been a visionary of the restaurant trade, but even he would have had to admit that we got there first. *Kitchen Confidential* was an expansion text based on Bourdain's 1999 *New Yorker* article *Don't Eat Before Reading This*. Richard had been penning such eating out injunctions for years, before Bourdain chanced along. And the conclusion in his *New Manchester Review* articles was always the same – most restaurant food shouldn't be served to your dog (or your cat!) They deserve better.

By the way, there was no evidence, no farewell note, to explain **why** Bourdain hanged himself on 8th June 2018, with his bathrobe belt in the bathroom of a five-star hotel in a converted 18th-century mansion in France. He was two weeks short of his 62nd birthday. The previous week, Bourdain and the TV crew for his CNN show had travelled to the medieval village of Kayserberg in northeastern France to film an episode on Alsatian food. LeChambard Hotel in Alsace, was the location for a shoot for his cable food and travel show, *Parts Unknown*.

Bourdain caught the media bang to rights when he exited this breathing world stage left. He hadn't come down for dinner to the hotel's rustic diner the previous evening, the first sign that something was in the air. "We thought it was strange," waiter Maxime Voinson told the *New York Times*, recalling Bourdain's no-show the night before his suicide.

Even Eric Ripert, Anthony Bourdain's close friend and host, thought something was amiss given that the pair had dined together pretty much every night at the hotel's quaint bistro, the Winstub, known for its foie gras and charcuterie.

Bourdain and Ripert had also eaten breakfast together each morning, again at the Winstub's big, distressed-wood tables. "They'd have fresh bread, Viennese pastries, panacota verrines, dried fruits," said the waiter of the hotel's breakfast offerings. "Dried fruits, cold cuts, local cheese, fruit salad, butter, honey and a jar of Christine Ferber jam."

And again, on Friday morning, Bourdain failed to join his host at the table. "His friend was waiting at breakfast," the waiter told the *New York Times*. "And waiting and waiting." Also waiting down the road, was Bourdain's camera crew.

Master butcher Christine Speisser told *People* magazine that the crew had set up to film at an outdoor market in nearby Strasbourg. Speisser was to show Bourdain around the market, starting at 10 a.m. Then a production assistant rushed to the scene, blurting out: "There's a big problem. It was like they were all struck by lightning," Speisser told *People*. "They all just sat on the ground."

An hour would pass. "They didn't say what was happening. They probably didn't know everything," Speisser's friend Christelle Schenck, who had been there to help with the filming, told *People*. Finally, "apparently, they need to cancel, we were told," Schenck said. "They said we'll call you back."

But call came there none. Back at the hotel, Bourdain wasn't picking up his cell phone. It was 9:30 a.m. and Ripert got up from his table at the Winstub, forsaking the breads, pastries and local cheeses he'd been set to share with his good friend.

And it was renowned French chef Ripert, the executive head honcho at Manhattan's famed Le Bernadin, who found Bourdain hanged in his bathroom that morning.

But June 8th, 2018, proved a bad day to film anything for *Parts Unknown*. Even on-site witnesses had struggled to capture the drama of the situation for the media. The reporters, too, had done their best. But they were never up close and personal. They never are, as any honest journo will tell you!

Even in a war zone, it is rare for a journalist to witness the actuality, the zonal iniquity, with their own eyes. Instead, they become night (and day) crawlers chasing down any witness who can tell them WTF just happened? This is especially true of a TV reporter who has to make a tricky, split-second decision about who to film – thus ... *"anyone here whose family has been killed by the latest drone strike, and speaks English?"*

So, on that rare occasion when the reporter is actually there, they can glory in a full house in spades.

"And that's just how was for me," says Rich, recalling the first time he met a Welsh wizard named Rovi at a restaurant quaintly called Quaintways in Chester in the mid-Swinging Sixties.

The two hit it off, sharing common knowledge of what went on in newspaper composing rooms in the days of hot metal (circa 1300!). Rovi was doing his close-up card tricks at the tables, and another performer was conjuring up a cabaret volcano right out of his mouth.

The fire-eater, who called himself Stromboli, managed to set off the ballroom sprinkler alarm system, and dozens of diners got an unexpected shower with their meal.

"No need for any witnesses, I saw it all," recalls Rich. And he found it all out, too! It turned out that Stromboli was no suave Italian from Milan, Turin or even Sicily, but an Irishman from north Manchester, who told Rich he'd warned Quaintways about the risk to the sprinkler alarms. Rovi said the management ignored Stromboli. You couldn't make this stuff up!

All that was 20 years before the spectral beast of Café Josie was stirring in the undergrowth. In that summer of 1986, the *New Manchester Review* restaurant reviews finally triggered the fantasy that was to become the theme diner called Café Josie.

If you've recovered your nerve after scanning this far and can guess what's coming down the track, read on voraciously – if you dare!

1 THE VANISHING

When you discount everything that's impossible Watson, what we have left no matter how improbable, is likely to be the truth.

SHERLOCK HOLMES

MANY BELIEVE THAT THE INDAN ROPE TRICK is the most unfathomable mystery that anyone has ever witnessed. And looking for answers down the years made the whole thing even more mysterious for Victoria's English Raj commissioners who were sent to investigate (taking their cue from an exclusive report in the *Chicago Tribune*).

They'd call at the village of a last reported sighting of the miracle, and the local head honcho would always have the same spiel: "Oh yes, sahib, Gunga Din was here, only yesterday, oh yes sahib. But he's gone now who knows where, oh yes sahib." Maybe they should have wired the Foreign Office to call in the guys from 221B Baker Street. (*"These Sepoys, Watson! It's money for old rope!"*)

But even Holmes would have been nonplussed about Café Josie's disappearance. I mean, how do you explain what happened? One moment there it was, a theme restaurant shimmering behind its all-encompassing black venetian blinds and its unmistakeable claim to being a 'restaurant cosmopolitain'! And the next, there's a shining Gujarati eatery right there in its place instead, with a dazzling green/blue neon sign board plain as a pikestaff, with a menu as long as your arm, complete with every Englander's favourite dish chicken tikka masala?

As the *Manchester Evening News* reported: "It was a venture where diners were entertained between courses by a table-touring conjuror with a pack of cards and other prestidigitator's accoutrements. And then, magically, shazam! the venue vanished altogether, and mysteriously turned into an Indian restaurant."

Indeed, it was a metamorphosis so fast and so complete, that even the Great Houdini would have been impressed. And he'd have known all about lightning-fast changes. His substitution-trunk illusion was right up there as the fastest on record, he used to claim.

But, of course, what really made Houdini's name was escapology. And a razor-sharp American producer of roadshows saw that what really engaged audiences was Houdini's nightly escape from regulation police handcuffs clicked on by a real live cop, right up there in the glare of the footlights. Houdini took the producer's advice and started devising other imaginative ways of escaping restraints, straitjackets, packing crates, water torture cells.

And in the late summer of 1900 Houdini took an ocean liner to England and the rest, as they say, is history. Houdini toured all over Europe in that first decade of the 20th century, escaping from packing cases, milk churns, and most famously, from the 'Chinese Water Torture Cell' where he was shackled upside down in glass-sided tank full of water. A legend was being born.

But, of course, our Erich secretly demurred at being lionised as the Handcuff King, when what he really wanted to be famous for was big stage illusions – like vanishing an elephant, which he pulled off on the New York Hippodrome stage in 1918. Even seasoned magicians were scratching their heads over how he did it, but he never let on. It was the elephant in the room that stayed grey in the shadows – like the beast that did for Café Josie a century later.

And yes, even seasoned magicians in 1989 were perplexed by the Café Josie enigma. But how, why? WTF! It's a conundrum that has exercised a growing coterie of interested bystanders – including discerning diners – over the last 30 years. And with mankind's latest new-fangled invention the Internet, the chorus has been growing ever more shrill. What the hell happened? Did we miss something? Did the Café vanish up Josie's sleeve? And hey Josie, when are you going to put us out of our misery, and reveal all?

Ok, I surrender! Welcome, to the denouement. It's been on my mind ever since the moment we vanished without trace all those years ago. Are you watching closely, because blink and you'll miss it! Like all those aficionados of haute cuisine did at the end of those two shining years in the late eighties, as the MADchester decade drew to a close.

The Café Josie project came out of that *Boys from the Blackstuff* moment when we thought, we could do that – and a lot better, too! (Blackstuff moment, Gizza job! Google it!). Well, welcome to the crazies who did it, and lived to tell the tale which is unfolding now before your very eyes. Two ordinary people, a British middle class couple living the dream! Whoah!

There was no groundbreaking theory behind the genesis of Café Josie's USP – table-top conjuring between courses. We scarcely knew anything about the way they did it in the US of A. It was pure, unadulterated guesswork, wishful thinking. An idea that materialised on a wing and a prayer, you might say. That magic theme only really kicked in after we'd opened, and we were looking for reasons to defend the whole idea to the Press – and to diners.

It started slow, but long before the end was near, Friday and Saturday nights were fully booked up weeks in advance. And casual drop-in diners had no chance. We learnt a lot fast. How to deal with party groups of eight/10/12 diners and how to factor in the magicians between courses to ease things for the kitchen. It meant that diners began staying for two/three hours and didn't wanna go home even then, when they'd long finished their meal.

Within months of opening, we were hosting big party celebrations, 16-20 people, sometimes two such groups on one night. We were overwhelmed. It didn't occur to us that it wasn't just the magic and the quality of the food that people were coming for. But also the fact that it was all so reasonably priced – and a bargain for a whole night out like no other!

And the magic was dazzling and free! We had 50 covers – as dining places are called in the biz – but the fact that we couldn't turn tables (i.e., get two sittings from each table) on a night, was the elephant in the room. A grey shadow, but an elephant nonetheless. But we went on, oblivious to the shadow looming in the background, so intoxicated were we by the effect we were having on our paying customers.

It had all started off alarmingly quietly on a late Summer evening in 1987. There'd been a thunderstorm that September Tuesday afternoon, a portent of things to come, obviously. Well, there we were, bright-eyed and bushy tailed, nervously rarin' to go, and not one booking that evening to look forward to.

I'll never forget that first night – we'd come back from the market and then it was into the kitchen, and a quick change into chefs whites as the day's preparations began. The butcher delivered on time and our main chef Kim prepped the fish and the meat. I made the soup, and prepped the rest of the starters, except the pate – this was Kim's recipe and so I took notes to make sure it would always be as good as this first one.

Our delightful chief waitress aka Maîtresse D' Hedda arrived and laid the tables with her famous fan napkins. To be honest that first night was a bit of a blur, I was running on adrenalin, but we survived! I was exhausted, so was everyone else. We'd be relying on walk-ins, the sort of people who liked driving past Europe's biggest municipal cemetery.

Rich had insisted there was no way he could do the magic – he'd just help out with the Maître D' role. So, we booked a young magi from Manchester Met's recent Magic Aid Convention, guy by the name of Tony Brooks, complete with shiny, spangled coloured jacket that screamed something strange this way comes.

That first night, we had three tables of four and two pairs, all walk-ins, all night. The couples were the kind of a diners who are star-crossed lovers and just wanna hold hands as they caress their glasses of wine and look into each other's eyes. Being asked to pick a card didn't look quite the thing to take their eyes off each other, as Tony had quickly sussed.

What happened next was unbelievable. So, he brazenly walks over to one of the couple's tables and asks to borrow a £10 note, in the sort of stentorian voice that made Dick Turpin's reputation. The bloke looked up stunned. But he handed over the tenner with just a hint of malice in his eyes, as Tony inquired in an officious tone of voice: "Is there anything fishy about this note?"

He held it up to the light in mock examination, casting doubt on its provenance and then, without further ado, he swiftly rolled it up and poured out a live goldfish into a glass of water. The couples' irritation at having their bliss interrupted vanished to be replaced with gasps of astonishment. Tony unrolled the £10 note and returned it to Mr Dreamlover, as he reached into his jacket for his wallet.

"I don't normally keep goldfish about me, as I don't carry any money. Just these magazine cut-out pictures of sports cars," Tony announces. And he flashes and counts off the six pieces of paper, one by one. "It's safer, in case of pickpockets. But if I need some of the real stuff, I just conjure it up like this!"

And instantaneously, the bundle of car pictures morphs into a bunch of crisp new tenners. Just like that! Well, the couple were really onside now, and Tony spent another five minutes at their table with an invisible deck of cards, which somehow just materialised out of thin air. By 10, the four-tablers and romantic dining couples had left, and we closed the doors.

Now all the staff would be fed and watered with a late dinner and drinks from the bar. Tony, too, as it was with all guest magi throughout the time of Café Josie. Tony repaid the compliment and put on a show for staff at the end of the meal. A perfect end to a rather depressing first night. (Cheers Tony, later Tony Rix due to Equity actors union protocol)

Then we had to do it all again! We now had the formula and just needed the stamina to keep going. (Luckily, Tony Brooks was available for a couple of more spots. And we booked in another Magic Aid magi by the name of John Hotowka, as I recall.)

You have to love cooking to do it for a living, and fortunately our main chef Kim and I both loved it. But I hadn't realised how hard it is during service when the waitress comes in with the first check, and then it's a whirlwind of teamwork during service to get that food out of the kitchen to the high standard we both demanded, and super-fast.

The rest of the week was much the same. Wednesday & Thursday came and went, and Friday, too. Average number of diners per night perhaps a dozen, with maybe double that number on Friday. It could have been a few more, but not many. Not good business, but a perfect run-in for our kitchen brigade. Which was perhaps just as well. Our main man chef Kim was still settling in – fortunately untroubled at having to defer to his fellow female chef (who, of course, happened to be his employer). The rest of the brigade comprised a sous chef Donna, a student at the local catering college on work experience, and a hardy washer-up.

But it's worth pointing out if you're tempted to go down this path, remember Bourdain's injunction that any chef worth his salt is an absolute dictator, a martinet! He cares passionately about anything that goes out of HIS kitchen! Napoleon? the Pharaohs? Pussycats by comparison.

Our big stroke of genius for the third week, was to place a story and advert in the north Manchester *Jewish Gazette* which came out on a Thursday. It was recommended by our solicitor Tony Lyons, an upstanding member of Manchester's renowned Jewish community, who was fielding our application for an alcohol licence, without which we'd opened. It was a case of bring your own bottle of wine for the first couple of weeks.

But at the end of that third week, a terrible beauty was born. It's called a reality check. Ok, by the time Saturday came, we were fully booked. We knew the advert had been a stroke of genius by the number of phone calls we fielded all day Friday. Saturday night was gonna be a full house, and we were still turning away would-be diners all day Saturday.

But, but . . . I'm getting ahead of myself! How the kitchen materialised at all for our first opening night is the kind of elevator pitch that Hollywood thrillers are made of, and it came in a veritable crescendo of flashing light bulbs. It was a moment to die for, a moment when everything you believed was turned on its head! That matrix moment, when you realised you'd been living in a dream world!

Even before those first, historic opening nights, the kitchen needed sorting Bourdain style, and there was to be no pussyfooting around!

Magicians called to the bar

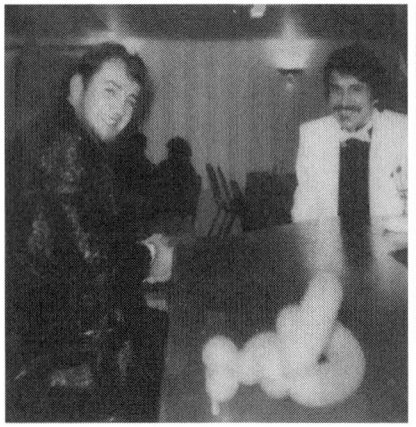

Balloon dog gets in a twist (left) with Tony Brooks and Rich Adamson; and (above) looking as suave as ever, Peter Clifford

Bamboozled at the table by two Daves

Asked to pick a card by masters of legerdemain Dave Allen (right) and Dave Jones (below), you've no chance!

2 TOTAL RECALL

*If I were you, I'd get your ass to
Mars or I'll die wondering.*

SECRET AGENT DOUG QUAID TO
ARNOLD SCHWARZENEGGER

IT WAS THE LATE, GREAT NAPOLEON Bonaparte who averred that a victorious army marches on its stomach. (That, and closely enfiladed, mobile light artillery, of course).

The Corsican corporal's paramour would have heartily agreed, given that she shared his affection for the glories of the dinner table plate with her wonderfully tasty cooking. Of course, a hearty meal sees all the blood and energy rushing to your stomach, leaving the gluttonous eater quite drowsy. And incapable, in the congress department, to boot! Hence, Boney's famous remark "Not tonight, Josephine".

Whoah! Hold on dear reader, don't write my publisher and me a snotty letter saying I'm making it all up! Just Google it, and you'll get the picture. Of course, I'm embroidering the actuality for effect (just as Jane Austen advised), and that's why you've read so far. It's a great story. And believe me, there's a lot more where that came from, and it's the kind of stuff that even Hollywood wouldn't dare make up.

So, get real, pay attention as I tell all. The big fact was we had a dream, yeah, a dream! And however different from Martin Luther's personal vision, it was this defining reality that presaged the action that followed. You think it first, mull it over, look out across your personal patch of this world, and say why not?

Hang on in there! The fact is that, sociologically speaking, it's every Brit middle class couple's wet dream to set up their own little restaurant! Check it out, ask around, think about it yourself. Admit it, you did too, once! Yup, up 80 per cent of us at one time or another, according to social surveys, have dreamed this wet dream. But most of us never get around to actually doing anything about it. Do we? We have second thoughts, we'd be mad to, wouldn't we! A wave of being sensible, being realistic, comes over most of us.

So, where did this wriggling worm of an idea come from, and how did it start burrowing its way into our mushy dream brains? Well, it's quite simple really. We were regularly dining out! So, there we were, sitting at our umpteenth restaurant table in a month across Greater Manchester, thinking how the hell do they get away with serving up this kind of trash?

You see, I was the dining companion of the man who was the Eating Out correspondent for *New Manchester Review* back in the lazy, hazy, crazy days of the late 70s. And I had to agree with Rich's oft barbed remarks that he wouldn't feed most menu offerings to our Shih Tzu. (that's a Japanese lap dog).

Richard and I ate out regularly and he would write a piece for the *New Manchester Review* under the name Josh Rogan. We never let any restaurant know we were reviewing them and more often than not, we were disappointed.

They just don't know how to cook! he'd say. Not nearly was as good as you! Your spaghetti bolognese is to die for, and your home-made beef burgers would put McDonald's out of business! Cue slight blush to the cheeks, and a waved head of "nah" denial on my part.

And so, it went on, month after month, year after year. But we didn't do nowt! How could we? It wasn't realistic. We couldn't. It was just a fantasy. The only people getting their money's worth were the discerning readers of *New Manchester Review*, for whom the five-star eatery review was their go-to-first reading. You remember those honeyed words framed with a five-star verdict? Yup, that was the genesis of everything that came after.

Fast forward 10 years, and a chunk of newspaper redundancy cash (courtesy the *Daily Express*) lands in my companion's lap. And suddenly it's wet dream time all over again. This time we have the readies to do it. Yeah, but we can't just set up any old eatery, it has to have something else, something very special. Like with entertainment. A Spanish guitar player, perhaps. Yeah, that sounds ok, if a bit cheesy, we thought. A romantic serenade with strings as you eat your noodles! Then came that brain explosion moment, that makes for the best Hollywood movies!

You're shaking your head in disbelief? Well, the first thing to say is that very few (if any) restaurants we visited had complementary entertainment with the meal. So, we had nothing to go on. Oh, there as one place that had a balalaika trio, a Greek joint as I recall. It was embarrassing. No! We needed something else.

So, came that light bulb moment! How about some conjuring tricks on the dining table between courses? It's your hobby, Richard! You entertain the whole family every Christmas after the Xmas puds have been served! He thought about it for a nanosecond, then airily dismissed the whole idea as a wet dream too far.

On second thoughts, I had to agree, and thought no more about it. But a week later, Rich mentions a magicians' charity gathering was taking place in Manchester next month, and he thought he might pop down to see what's what. He goes to the Magic Aid Convention at Manchester Metropolitan Uni a few Sundays later and comes back with stars in his eyes. He says he's met an old friend from his days as a Chester newspaper journalist. Man with a funny name, Rovi!

Rich explains Rovi is a Welsh guy whose real name is Ivor Parry. He'd first met Rovi at Chester's Quaintways Restaurant where he was appearing at a dinner he was writing up for the *Cheshire Observer*. They reported that sort of thing in those days (late Sixties). He'd watched Rovi go round the tables – including his own – with just a pack of cards and a cheeky, mischievous grin. And he'd been amazed at the reaction Rovi got, but he didn't give it a second thought.

Rich got chatting with Rovi, and they hit it off because he was a fellow newspaper man from North Wales – a print supervisor in the composing room of the *Caernarfon Herald* in those hot metal days. And that was that. This was the Swinging Sixties, and restaurant reviewing was far away in the distant future. And Rich never imagined he'd ever meet Rovi again. Of such stuff are all our dreams made.

But there at the Magic Aid Convention was Rovi, who remembered Rich as if they'd met only the day before, and they got talking. Apparently, Rich mentioned to Rovi he was planning to open a new *theme* restaurant, would Rovi be interested? Rovi said that although he lived in Caernarfon – which is as far away from Manchester as you can get without falling into the Irish Sea – he would come to Manchester. And he'd love to do a spot at our restaurant when it opened.

My God! If only I'd known! That's when Rich dropped his bombshell! Tabletop conjuring would be a great idea, like we said, but he personally couldn't do it! I said, whadya mean you can't do it? You pull the rabbits out of the hat at every Christmas party (true). The family love it (also true).

Then Rich explained that what he did wasn't magic, and he'd never get away with that kind of stuff close-up on a dining table. What's more, the kind of stuff real magicians did close-up, he couldn't do. He hadn't a clue! He'd decided after seeing the performers at Magic Aid, that he'd have to start all over again. Whoah!

So here we are setting up a *magic themed* restaurant, and the main man doesn't have a clue how it's done. Are you sure we should be doing this, I ask? Rich nods, smiles and says I can't wait to watch and learn. You perform the magic in the kitchen, and I'll be out front, scoping out every magician's sleight-of-hand from the legendary Hofzinser's spread cull to Ammar's invisible bill switch, to the miraculous Mercury Card Rising! Ya just gimme the goodies from your bank of woks, baby!

And that's when a second brain explosion went off – this time all in my own head! Me work the magic in the kitchen? In your dreams – and mine! OK, I could cook for sure – I had learned a lot from my first husband's Italian family. But to cook for a full house of 50 discerning diners for real? Every night? There was no way that I could do that. No way!

And what T F were we going to serve up to our hungry diners? Boiled beef 'n' carrots just didn't cut the mustard! Not even my own Spag Bog! We needed a menu to die for, and then some. And where was that gonna come from! And where was the chef who could deliver such wonders?

That's when a fairy princess on a dappled grey horse came riding to the rescue.

3 TRANSFIXING DA VINCI

*The universe is mind-bending and
reality is not what it seems.*

CARLO ROVELLI,
THEORETICAL PHYSICIST OF LOOP QUANTUM GRAVITY

ENGLAND'S LEGENDARY LANDSCAPE GARDENER Lancelot Capability Brown, renowned for redesigning Mansfield Park with his arboreal transplant miracles, would have had a neatly trimmed rejoinder for any fantasist who believed that restaurants grew on trees. "They don't! Imbecile!" (He would have been gobsmacked to learn restaurants have grown very well on trees. For example, check out Tree House Restaurant & Café Monteverde Costa Rica; and many more amazing Treehouse Restaurants: https://theculturetrip.com/central-america/costa-rica/articles/amazing-treehouse-restaurants-around-world/)

But even Capability Brown would have gone gaga over the impossibly tall line of gently swaying poplars across the road acting like Arcadian sentinels to oblivion, right opposite the rundown parade of shops where it all began. The scene conjured up an eerie foreboding '*et in Acadia ego sum*'.

'Black poplars' were known to tolerate the air pollution created by factories burning vast amounts of coal across Greater Manchester. At the time these majestic trees* shaded the boundary of the largest municipal cemetery in Europe that extends all along the edge of Barlow Moor Road, Chorlton-cum-Hardy, Manchester. (*Many of these poplars were felled after 2000 because of an airborne fungus - poplar scab disease [*Venturia populina*])

So, it was on that fateful day in early 1987, having driven a short way along Barlow Moor Road, we joined the estate agent parked on the forecourt to the double-fronted showroom of a former carpet shop. Above there was five-bed living accommodation and at the rear, a spacious yard.

Well, it looked great, but as Brown (1715-1783) would have said, it wasn't 'capable' of being a five-star eatery. For that, you had to dig it up, trees and all, and sculpt a terrible new beauty where Nature's laws could be bent. (Brown's visionary modus operandi was uprooting and relocating mature trees, a trademark feat of arboreal engineering. And Jane Austen would have appreciated the allusion to Mansfield Park!)

We'd been hunting for months for suitable premises in which to launch our dream, and there had been some near (bad) misses – too big, too small, no parking, rubbish location, etc.

One particularly absurd close call was with a corner premises we'd found on Burton Road in West Didsbury. We'd put in a planning application to the City Council for a change of use to 'Josie's Bistro" (fully licensed, of course), which was reported in the local paper. Residents objected, prompting the triumphal headline 'Ahaa, Bistro No!" The application was turned down. So that was that.

But this place looked absolutely right, although we had some doubts about the location. But if you ignored the cemetery – which you could as it was screened by poplars all along a main road – it was ideal. Now we needed to work our own transplant miracle.

The premises were not only roomy and in good condition, but even had parking space for a dozen cars on a spacious forecourt in front of the showroom. And it had been vacant for a good six months, so the agent was keen for a sale! The premises were in such good shape, clean, with overhead lighting, that the price seemed like a giveaway – £46,000 for the freehold.

We'd sell our house, and we could move in above right away with our daughter Danielle then aged two – everything was so clean, tidy and spacious, with full central heating. All the work that needed doing was downstairs, where we would transform the front showroom and ancillary back storage areas into the dining room and purpose-fitted cooking area – a powerhouse kitchen. Simple. Then, the project's first landmine exploded.

It was only while we were checking the details of the freehold contract with our solicitor Tony Lyons that we discovered the premises were covered by a usage covenant held by Manchester City Council. That covenant had been passed down to the public authority by the previous owner who quite likely had been a god-fearing, temperance sort of guy. He might be a long time dead, but he didn't want his earthly abode used for boozing when he was gone. Specifically, licensed premises was not a permitted activity.

Shell-shocked? We felt like the Light Brigade charging all those dug-in Russian guns; there seemed no way we'd get out alive! That's when our brief came to the rescue. Apparently, Tony Lyons had dealt with this kind of thing before while fielding planning applications, and he was confident the City Council would waive the covenant provided it didn't clash with any other change-of-use ordinance, from A2 retail to A3 sale of foodstuffs, etc.

But there was a sting in the tail. The council asked for a waiving fee of £5,000, agreed of course, towards public funds, ditto. The cost of nulling the covenant was a major setback as it ate into our budgeted funds. (The lesson being, always factor in a 25% -plus cushion for the unexpected!) Most of our budgeted funds were earmarked for carrying out extensive alterations to the inside of the building as well as the frontage which, of course, would be our signpost to the world that was driving by. We'd planned an ambitious bells and whistles display with our name in neon lights for the frontage. But, alas, it was not to be.

We'd run out of money and thus had to settle for a very modest name sign of silver, stick-on letters applied to the overpainted dramatic pitch black on the existing signboard. It was very, very low key, most unprepossessing, even gloomy. Hardly an engaging invitation to sample the magic of miracles on your plate as well as on your tabletop!

However, our masterstroke to compensate for the dour exterior signboard, was to encase the inside of the plate glass showroom window in black venetian blinds. And we wrapped the interior neon ceiling lights in soft pink filters, so looking into the restaurant, even from quite a distance, presented a vision of a rosy-tinted mystery palace.

Fixing the inside proved to be far less problematic than we'd thought. The place could comfortably seat 50 diners and there were swing doors immediately connecting to the spacious kitchen area and storage rooms behind. And it was already fitted throughout with showroom lighting. All that was needed was a doubling up of the wiring electrics, refitted to conform to safety regulations for licensed premises.

For the rest, it was largely cosmetic, not too formidable, and tasks for which we'd budgeted. The main tasks that needed doing were equipping the kitchen and the installation of toilet facilities for men and women. (My brother-in-law Colin Meek did wonders with plumbing and electrics in record time).

Our carpenters built a very chic, dark wood bar area to our own spec, and installed ladies and gents around it. And we made sure one could eat Christmas dinner on the loo even if caught short in the ladies – or the gents! The condition of restaurant toilets during our *New Manchester Review* days had been an obsession with both Rich and me. We reasoned that customers could judge what went on behind closed doors in the kitchen by the condition of the place's toilets. (We found out later that it had also been one of Anthony Bourdain's signature tests of an eatery's credentials.)

Richard and I agreed that male facilities should be ultra clean, bright and functional, but that things would be more pampering, feminine and comfortable for the ladies. There was double vanity sink, and blusher-pink wallpaper above tiling in black and gold, and soft carpeting. And big bouquets of fresh flowers. To top it off, on the ladies door was a big picture of the Mona Lisa. (I wonder what Da Vinci would have made of his masterwork portrait signposting the ladies?) The gents made do with the Laughing Cavalier!

On the booze front, we located a brewery who agreed to supply the bar with lager, beer and cider on tap and a selection of wines, mostly French and Italian. They were also able to supply a very reasonable house wine, red and white, which they customised with Café Josie supply-printed labels, no less. But there are many wine merchants among whom trade is very competitive, so a good deal is always possible.

We had the wine cellar behind the kitchen. We couldn't afford to get it professionally fitted out so bought those plastic wine holders that hold six bottles. And as there was no central heating, we could also stash crates of bottles on the floor. My office was also in there, a bit chilly, not ideal, but needs must.

And then came the kitchen area, the engine room, the beating heart of the enterprise, where there was no room for mistakes. I'd decided that everything had to spotless and subject to instant wipe-cleansing at any moment. So, we decided on white ceramic tiles from floor to ceiling on every wall. The kitchen area was basically a mess, and I knew it could only be transformed to meet hygiene standards by tiling. (Luckily, Richard's brother Patrick had just came back from India, and was absolutely brilliant. I think he tiled the whole kitchen area virtually by himself!).

Choosing the name for our new eatery proved to be an annoyingly elusive task. Try it some time, and you'll see what I mean. We came up with all sorts of names, Magic Café, Mystery Bistro, Rick's Café (yeah, eat your heart out, *Casablanca*). And all the while we were dressing up the identity of our new eatery as if it were a Parisian bistro – thus restaurant cosmopolitain.

We knew Joséphine de Beauharnais became Empress of France, but what the hell were we doing? Then suddenly Café Josie appears just like that! Whoah! (The fact that the proprietor's name was Josephine played no part in naming the restaurant … duh! Gimme a break Warden!)

But perhaps we were afraid, uncertain, anyone would take such an eatery seriously if it had magic in the name. Conjuring with catering was big news in USA, but not in UK! We were gonna do something never done before! So, choosing the name came to be at the heart of the matter. (What would any of our stable of magicians have come up with? It's harder than it looks!) So, Café Josie it was. And it stuck coz we were running out of options, not to say time.

Then the second landmine exploded. The powers-that-be were scheduled to carry out an on-site visit to see that everything they'd approved under planning regulations had been complied with. Everything including the kitchen had to be ready for the visit of the

City Council's licensing committee – all dozen members – and reps from police and fire services. And magistrates. I kid you not!

It was going to be a close-run thing, but we were determined to pull it off, including the engine room the kitchen. I'd decided Café Josie cooking would be derived from wok-based cooking ranges. Flash-fry and stir-fry would be perfect for what I wanted to provide, which was fusion-based (East and West) dishes cooked in record time!

I'd even managed to summon a gallant, 7th Cavalry horsewoman, to help capture a real-life chef reading from the same cookbook, who was gonna head up my brigade in the kitchen (perhaps not such a good analogy, considering Custer's fate). But I had to thank my good personal friend Liz Howells (who has sadly passed away), for the inspired choice of chef. She was a fine horsewoman with her own grey steed which she kept in farm stables a couple of miles from her flat. And she knew I was having kittens about Café Josie.

How was I, a total amateur, going to work any magic in the kitchen, all on my ownsome, cooking every night, for discerning diners for real, and where was that menu to die for? (Gulp!) It's what Anthony Bourdain called the dark recesses of a restaurant underbelly – a sub-culture whose centuries-old militaristic hierarchy and ethos of 'rum buggery and lash' make for a mix of unwavering orders and nerve-shattering chaos! (And you still wanna open that pretty little diner of yours sometime soon?)

We knew from our *New Manchester Review* days, that most diners put up with indifferent fare, poor service and high prices, because dining out is usually for a special occasion, a celebration. Restaurant patrons tend to be people who have invested a lot of emotional energy in having a good time, no matter what the circumstances. That's the reason why most UK eateries stay in business long past their sell-by date. (Bourdain reckoned that in his day, there was a 60% failure rate among New York restaurants)

But a *Menu Meister* was on the way. My fairy princess on the dappled grey-white charger didn't let me down. Liz suggested that we go eat at a pub brasserie in nearby Didsbury and sample the chef's offerings there. She did part-time waitressing there and knew the chef, Kim, personally. She was keen to see what I thought about his cooking.

The moment I started on my soup of the day, I thought Liz was having me on. The leek broth tasted gritty, and as I bit into my Thai Salad Special a tiny live snail was wriggling at the bottom of the bowl! The service was indifferent, the food utterly memorable for the wrong reasons. Liz looked baffled and called the waiter over. She asked to speak to her friend the chef Kim Merritt, only to be told it was his night off. We're gonna have to come back, she said simply. I didn't know whether to laugh or cry. Ok, I said, tomorrow, counting down the hours to our opening night.

Well, to cut a long story short, we duly rolled up next evening and ate our fill of Kim's own menu, and I was in ecstasy! Really. After service was done, we stayed and Kim came out washed-up, for a beer at the bar and a chat with his good friend Liz – and me. That's when I realised that the restaurant business is a fiercely protective, closed world of its own, where nothing happens by chance or surprise (just as Bourdain said).

Kim said he was curious about our new venture and wished me luck. That's when I hit him full-on with the offer that one can't refuse. Do you wanna head up my brigade? Kim glanced at Liz and it was agreed. We arranged to meet next day at the Café, and suddenly I was on Cloud Nine as our dream looked to becoming a reality.

It all seemed very rosy, but there was a fly in the ointment. The last thing Kim said as we left to go was "what's all this stuff about magicians on the tables?" with the expression of a man facing the firing squad! And I thought, oh no! It's always the devil in the detail that bites you on the bum!

4 PLATE TECTONICS

Those who think they know everything are a great annoyance to those of us who do.

ISAAC ASIMOV

CLAIRVOYANTS AND AFICIONADOS OF SCI-FI film and tv thrillers like *Quatermass and the Pit* will know that Old Nick never wore Prada or ever needed to wrap up in disguise (pace Elvis!). You have only to seek, and you'll find him around any thoroughfare that bears his name.

It was during domestic science class that I first encountered the aroma of garlic, herbs and spices, whose names I didn't know, and the diabolical individual whose unearthly presence I thought was downright spooky. And my teacher Miss Hobbs did little to assuage such impressions, deploying a booming voice and the faintest trace of an acid smile while instructing our class. She airily dismissed me as someone with my head in the clouds. I was a girl who could never be expected to cook to professional standards, she told my parents.

Talk about the devil in disguise! She even screwed up my choice of meal for my GCE practical exam, insisting I do a breakfast for four, instead of my first choice of a dinner party menu. But with my Scottish Granny's help, I smuggled in a Scottish breakfast - kedgeree (the origin is Indian) with Scottish oat pancakes and honey. Well, the devilish Miss Hobbs was not expecting that!

But despite that, I left school with my love of cooking undiminished and at 16 trained in silver service with the Co-op as a Saturday girl, working on weddings mostly. That gave me an insight into just how hard it was to work in catering which, in those days, was a male-dominated activity in a kitchen environment full of shouting and abuse, and uncannily close to Bourdain's insider underbelly.

Thus did this sweet innocent hook up with an armed and dangerous denizen of Bourdain's *Kitchen Confidential*, a real-life chef called Kim Merritt. Here we were in a Devil's Kitchen for sure, him breathing professional know-how like a hungry dragon and me gabbling wok-fusion cooking creativity of the kind Bourdain warned could lead to death by a thousand kitchen-knife cuts.

As Anthony Bourdain put it, the last thing that the main man Chef wants is a brigade cook who's an innovator with ideas of their own so they can mess around with Chef's recipes and presentations. No!

"They want near-fanatical loyalty and automaton-like consistency of execution under battlefield conditions."

Hallelujah! Well, suffice to say we – I and my new main man chef Kim – came to an accommodation, obviously, or I wouldn't be talking to you now. I suspect it was because Kim was still shell-shocked about the "magic theme" out front. He was desperately trying to come to terms with what it entailed. And he didn't want to let down his good friend Liz.

So, how did I get Kim totally on side amid all the talk of abracadabra? At another "summit" meeting of course, where both Richard and I spelled out what the Café Josie Magic Circle involved. He sat stony-faced, while Richard explained in detail what close-up conjuring at the tables meant. Kim's immediate response was that all this magic mullarkey would detract from his expertise in the kitchen – his food should be enough to satisfy customers without conjuring tricks!

Richard patiently explained magic would be performed after diners had made their first and main course choices. The magic would fill the time gaps – between order and service – while I prepared their starters, and Kim did the same for main courses.

Gradually, Kim felt a little easier as it became clear what this table-top legerdemain was all about. It was something he had never witnessed before, but I knew he would be blown away actually seeing some magic close-up himself.

So, there I was with a rough diamond in tow on the brink of the middle-class dream. But remember, if you're going with the dream, any chef worth his salt is an absolute dictator who cares passionately about anything that goes out of HIS (or HER) kitchen!

Kim was passionate about food, a trait I recognised. He liked to break the rules and not stick to any conventional idea of what any cuisine should be. I liked his ideas, and we spent some time talking them through. He liked my idea of a cosmopolitan, fusion menu, and we discussed at length how we'd go about creating dishes, a specials board and, more importantly, that we would 'cook to order'.

Showing him around the kitchen I told him I wanted a wok stand (unheard of outside a Chinese kitchen). I said we could get a double and also a conventional cooker. Kim, now onside, said he knew of a stainless-steel table going begging from a restaurant where he used to work. We went to meet the owner who was glad to see it go as it was already outside at the back of his premises, and pickup was arranged.

We measured for a double wok stand and a standard 6-burner cooker with oven and warm cupboard, plus an industrial microwave on a steel stand next to the cooker. And there was a serving counter at the other side of the 'dirty area' of the kitchen. Also, a double sink, table for drop-offs, used plates, etc. and an industrial dishwasher from a company I used to work for.

Opposite the cooker in a spur room backing off the main area, were the fridges and deep freezers. There was also a working counter, adjacent to the cooker. But starting out, the whole kitchen area was a mess. We knew it had to be tiled from floor to ceiling to meet hygiene standards, which I was obsessively keen on. Rich's brother Patrick was absolutely brilliant and completed the tiling in record time.

Out front we made positive important choices. We also wanted table linen, but not white. Dusky pink patterned tablecloths with a grey overlap were ideal and, of course, real napkins. We found a wholesale crockery and glass supplier, who provided our perfect match, grey plates with a dark pink border. This was a family run company who were very helpful with their advice, and we got the right cutlery and other kitchen items.

As for atmosphere decor out front, we opted for real plants to give it that *Casablanca* feel, so it had to be parlour palms. We decided to rent them and researched suppliers to find the right plants and planters. These weren't to be delivered until the last minute. But once in place they softened the whole tone of the atmosphere, giving it that "play it again, Sam" feel.

Over the next few weeks, Kim would pop in regularly to see how things were going and we got to work on ideas for our menu. I wanted at least one vegetarian dish (unheard of 30 years ago!). Kim was unsure about that – he liked his steak French blue! In his own words, it was "grab it by the horns, wipe its arse, stick it on the plate!" Well, I wasn't sure about that! But at least we agreed on a division of labour.

We decided I'd prepare and serve the starters, Kim the main courses. We decided on a small, easy-to-control menu: beef, pork, chicken, fish, vegetarian, with side orders of a selection of fresh vegetables, potatoes (mashed, dauphinois, sautéed), rice (basmati) and a tight dessert menu. Everything had to be fresh, and cooked in-house, with no additives or preservatives – fresh food, no bought-in, ready-made sauces, mayonnaise or pate, everything cooked from scratch. This was an exciting challenge.

Kim and I went to Manchester's famous Smithfield Market where he introduced me to Brian at J. W. Wilde and Sons, purveyors of fish. Brian took a liking to me and agreed to sell us smaller than usual amounts of fish (fresh, remember, we weren't going to freeze it) if we came to the market to get it, as it wouldn't be cost effective for them to deliver. And that was agreed. Next, we found a vegetable supplier that would provide the same service.

That done, Kim and I were satisfied the Great Café Josie menu could now be achieved. Kim and I used our knowledge to devise dishes that we could easily cook to order. We came up with a marinade for the lamb dish after trial and error to stop the sauce from splitting. I conjured up the spicy (very) chicken Szechuan and the vegetarian splendour of 'jewels of the night'. And so it went with every item on the menu we were devising.

We decided we'd always put the fish dishes on the Specials Board, based on what we had bought that day at market. We practised creating the dishes until we were satisfied, they would work. We needed to prep vegetables on the day and then cook, arrest and cool, ready to blast in the industrial microwave. Desserts were discussed and it was agreed they would include my signature cheesecake. Tasty!

Further on the equipment front, I sourced an industrial dishwasher from guy I used to work for. I won't use his name because he got me a duck egg, and I had to get someone else to fix it.

It's crazy how people you know can let you down. That was just one of the headaches, but a minor one. Out front we had a miracle with staffing to compensate. We needed a front of house co-ordinator of waiting-on staff. A mesmerising organiser.

I was going to be second chef, so needed a guardian angel to come along. And she did, in the form of Hedda. We had advertised for staff and Richard had taken a call from her and booked her in for interview straight away. I was a bit annoyed as it was such short notice – I had a million and one things I needed to do.

He convinced me saying: "If this girl looks anything like her voice, she's hired." Hmm, I was even more annoyed (no joking). I was tired and totally stretched out by what I still needed to do. I was sitting by the window laying out one of the tables as she came in. And whoah! What a vision greeted my eyes. Here was this Hedda, a tall, dark-haired, beautiful girl with an amazing smile who approached me so confidently, holding out her hand as she said: "Hello, how are you? I'm Hedda."

She was bright, confident, funny and so easy to talk to. She was hired. Hedda and I became good friends, but that's another story. (She passed away shortly after we closed due to illness. I miss her greatly . . .)

But back to the heart of the matter, and the menu Kim and I fought like cats and dogs over . . . well, not quite, but yes . . . you know what I mean.

The Café Josie MENU TO DIE FOR

OPENERS
Stuffed tomatoes - 2 tomatoes stuffed with minced beef fillet, topped with blue cheese and grilled.
Pate de foie de volaille - our own pate of chicken livers, laced with cognac, served with toast and salad
Spare ribs (Italian style) - served with a spicy sauce

MERCURY RISING

Soupe de la maison - *home-made mushroom soup, served with a swirl of cream*
Nude prawns - *juicy cocktail prawns smothered in mayonnaise, served with vegetable crudités.*
'Melorange' constellation - *a delicious melange of marinated melon and orange segments in port.*
Gravlax - *freshly prepared salmon, marinated for 24 hours.*

MAINS

Chi Szechuan – *one of my signature dishes I invented to delight the taste buds of the hot 'n' spicy-loving fraternity, like Rich: strips of aromatic breast of chicken, wok-sauteed with mushrooms and green peppers, and finished in oyster sauce, fresh ginger and chilli, served with rice.*
Fillet Madagascar - *8oz of prime beef fillet cooked to your liking with garlic, white wine and green Madagascar peppercorns, de-glazed with brandy and finished with cream.*
Scottish salmon with dill - *fillet of fresh salmon, simply baked in butter with fresh dill.*
Macedonian lamb - *lean chunks of lamb marinated in yoghurt with paprika and turmeric, and sautéed in butter with garlic, onions and red peppers.*
Pork van Gustang - *whole pork fillet, sautéed in butter, covered with mozzarella & grilled until golden, served in a white wine & lemon juice sauce.*
Poulet de Pompadour - *succulent breast of chicken sautéed with mushrooms & artichoke hearts, in a creamy sauce.*
"Jewels of the Night" Vegetarian speciality - *Roasted peppers stuffed with chick peas and spices in an aromatic sauce.*
Selection of fresh vegetables in a dish, and potatoes of the day. Our dauphinois potatoes were always popular, as were the sautéed ones.
Also salads, including a mixed, spicy Thai salad and a Middle Eastern salad.

CLOSERS

Selection of sweets of the day – such as carrot cake, Josie's cheesecake, fresh fruit salad.

I think we were first in Manchester to have Cafétieres at the table. We had found an excellent coffee merchant because we wanted to serve top notch coffee. We had experienced inferior coffee so many times when reviewing restaurants.

Specials Board – *very popular, with dishes such as* **smoked salmon parcels, spicy chicken wings** *or house prepared gravlax. We often had* **mussels, scallops,** *fish of the day to include,* **bream, tuna** *etc.*

Also, occasionally our monster **King Kong Prawn** *concoction. And, of course,* **Lobster Thermidor**, *until I called time on serial, crustacean murder at 247/249 Barlow Moor Road.*

At this stage we did not have a vegetarian main course option, so I devised a spicy chickpea dish, which we called 'Jewels of the Night' for the specials board. We weren't sure how this would be received, it was 1987 after all. But no worries, it proved a very popular main course, and even Kim was impressed.

The last bit in the jigsaw puzzle was something that wouldn't have taxed Dan Brown's Professor of Symbology – the table linen! We decided to launder all the linen ourselves, or should I say my Mum was enrolled to do it all in the flat upstairs. She had agreed to become the cleaner; I needed someone I could trust.

As for those tantalising last few things that needed fixing the day before appearing in court to apply for the liquor licence, we were still finishing off the decorating and just about everything else the night before.

I remember staying up into the early hours, shattered, painting stuff here and there, helped by our lodger Jimbo, a newspaper colleague of Rich's at their newspaper *News on Sunday*, wondering if we would ever get it all done in time. Now I know what it felt like rearranging the deckchairs on the Titanic!

The following morning, we had laid all tables and set out the restaurant as best we could. There were still things that needed finishing off, but we had our fingers crossed. That's went the next hand grenade went off.

A front-line, panzer attack coach pulls up outside and out steps the Manchester City Council war party – licensing committee, magistrates, reps of fire and police, one by one. There must have been two dozen of them armed with assault-style clip-boards and biros. I felt faint with worry.

They went all around the restaurant, poking their noses in everywhere, inspecting everything. Then the chairwoman abruptly called a halt and said: "No, not ready!" Then they were gone! Just like that!

We were stunned. I still had to attend magistrates court the following day, which would be nerve-wracking, especially as I knew we were about to be refused the licence. Back at the restaurant, staff were waiting for the news. They were crestfallen at first.

I parked any surplus deckchairs and checked our King Kong prawns were ready to make someone's day. Yeah, really! Bourdain would have approved how well we dealt with our speciality seafood. His mantra was cook it fresh, serve it fresh. "I know how old most seafood is on Monday – about four or five days old!" he rasped. So, seafood was always on our Specials Board of the day.

Then I announced we were still opening as planned next night with 'bring your own wine' for a month, while we waited to reapply and gain our liquor licence.

There were sighs of relief all round and the smiles returned to the faces of all Café Josie staff, mobilised by the incomparable Hedda while we dug in and prepared for our opening night and our grand, long-awaited entrance on to the MADchester scene.

Rovi revels in big reveals

May the (classic) Force be with you. . . was the incomparable; Rovi's opening gambit, and (left) Rich gets the lowdown, up close and personal, with the master

5 STRIP CHEF NAKED

The English language with its elaborate generosity, distinguishes between the naked and the nude.

SIR KENNETH CLARK

NOW I KNOW HOW JAMIE OLIVER FELT when TV producers told him the title of the show that was to launch him on the road to stardom. And I fully understand his reaction – that NFW! was he gonna appear on-screen nude.

Whoah! Hold on Jamie, I can hear the smart-assed producer say, we don't actually mean naked, that's just a come-on for the great unwashed multitude – and their matronly housewives – in front of their TV sets stuffing their faces with crisps, to get 'em to watch. They'll probably think it's some blonde young hunk who's gonna come on and show them how to boil an egg and flip his hot sausage safely. Ho, ho, ho!

No, Jamie, we're billing you as the ultimate amateur chef, a cook who's got no qualifications, hasn't been to catering college or even been apprenticed to some bigshot chef in an all expenses paid eatery off Fleet Street. You'll have no complex recipes to confuse viewers, or fancy-dan cooking utensils to work your culinary miracles. No, it'll be just you with a bottle opener and your bare hands. Bare. Nude. Naked! Geddit?

Yeah, I got it. The description was a dead ringer for me. A home-loving, untrained domestic cook, who could rustle up a mean spag bog and home-minced Maccy D quarter pounder to die for. (Naked or not!) But what else? A super-crafted, hard-boiled egg? It didn't add up to a hill of beans – broad, runner or kidney, as they said in *Casablanca* when Bogie stumbled on his lines during filming.

There's no record that Anthony Bourdain ever stumbled on his lines while performing for the camera. And he certainly didn't while giving his verdict on a showbiz cooking rival called Jamie Oliver: "A hairless, blond rich guy who pretends he scoots around on a Vespa and cooks green curry for his mates."

Of course, Bourdain clocked that Oliver was just like him, a TV chef "so few people actually ate his food". And though the 'naked' referred to his 'simple, unadorned' food, "a great number of matronly housewives would like to believe otherwise". No wonder Bourdain wished he was a time traveller and "could go back and bully him at school".

Or maybe he'd have held off beating up Jamie after reading Kenneth Clark. The art historian in his book *The Nude* draws a distinction between naked and nude. "To be naked is to be deprived of our clothes" and the word implies an element of embarrassment being in that condition. The word nude, however, is without discomfiture but rather, in educated conventions, elevated to a form of art, quoth Clark.

The art critic John Berger in his book *Ways of Seeing* put it differently. "To be naked is to be oneself: to be nude is to be seen naked by others and yet not recognised for oneself. A naked body has to be seen as an object in order to be a nude."

However, in Laura Mulvey's *Visual and Other Pleasures*, the concept of the male gaze is described as a heterosexual, masculine gaze, where women are regarded as passive objects of male desire. But in this world of Post-Modern Feminist Liberalism, now was the time to subvert all that by dishing up Jamie Oliver with the bare essentials under a 'female gaze'... perhaps even attracting the gaze of the non-heteronormative as well. Relish the thought!

So, here I was with my main man (aka Rich) who also doesn't have much chest hair and doesn't cook, either. He's twiddling his playing cards saying he ain't no magician and he'll watch and learn while I slave over hot cooking stoves twirling my chef's hat!

Suddenly, the whole project of conjuring tricks on diners' tables seemed quite absurd. What most people knew about "magic" was Paul Daniels and David Copperfield on television . . . How on earth would the very idea be received by actual real-life diners? How would they react to having their attention diverted from slurping their mulligatawny soup with an invitation to watch a card trick?

Not all reviewers had been impressed by being ambushed at their Café Josie table by a magician. "Eating your meal inside Paul Daniels' cape that might be an acquired taste for some," quoth one perspicaciously, once the local Press cottoned on. "Indeed, the whole idea of magicians performing in a dining room – though apparently much-loved by the Americans – will be viewed as intrusive by some, and just plain naff by others," said another magisterially.

Suddenly *Meals with a Touch of Magic*! didn't seem such a magical refrain. But then it's not hard to see how ingrained prejudice can warp anyone's perspective on the panoply of wonders that life's infinite tapestry of possibilities holds. Conjuring, magic tricks had become so much old hat (even with no rabbits) in an age where every technological advance looks like real magic. And TV shows like *Britain's Got Talent* and *America's Got Talent* had long since relegated conjurors to the scrapbag of audition also-rans (**Final curtain for TV magicians**, *Independent* 10.03.09). Guided, of course by Simon Cowell himself.

Then an amazing thing happened. In a flash, legerdemain was back! Today, hardly a show goes by on TV without at least one, sometimes two wonder workers pushing the boundaries of what's possible. And Britain has caught up with America's wildly successful *Penn & Teller* franchise. Even Syco looks rueful, as magician after magician fools his pants off, leaving him scratching his head and mumbling incoherently that what he's just seen "may well be real magic". A quantum of entanglement, obviously!

Thus does the madness of crowds infect even the most cynically rational of humanity's breeding stock.

But when Café Josie launched, it seemed there was nowhere to go with such entertainment. Our magicians' approach would have to be to deal their cards with a whisper – not so much a waterfall shuffle as a valiantly pared-down Daley's Aces, so as not to bore diners who've seen it all before at Christmas with Johnny's conjuring set. Or so we told ourselves.

This gargantuan twist in popular taste has its counterpart in the catering biz. Today, cooks are queuing up to become famous for 15 minutes as celebrity chefs on TV shows like *Master Chef*. And young whippersnappers like Jamie Oliver and ageing experts like Gordon Ramsey are emulating Anthony Bourdain and turning cooking into pure, unadulterated showbiz.

Thus, failing restaurateurs are being inveigled to hang themselves out to dry on camera with tears in their eyes. And every enthusiastic amateur is being invited by producers to go centre-stage and provide some cheap, reality TV angst. *Strip chef naked* and get viewers squirming! And if the chefs don't crash and burn, they might just demonstrate, once and for all, that cooking is no big deal. Anyone can do it!

Or if they've attained enough celeb status, they get to push back – and give deranged producers a hard time. As did Mel Giedroyc and Sue Perkins in early 2020, when they quit *The Great British Bake Off* on Day One "after tears had left a bad taste".

The celebrity baking pair told the *Guardian* they'd quit because they feared producers wanted to make a more intrusive and crueller show than they were happy with. The pair were due to start a seven-series run as hosts of the cookery show but resigned on the first day of filming.

As Sue Perkins told the *Radio Times*: "We resigned, basically, because it was not a kind show. They were pointing cameras in the bakers' faces and making them cry and saying, 'Tell us about your dead gran.' So, we had very stiff words about how we wanted to proceed. I think we can say that, now we're out of it, can't we?"

Mel and Sue's chemistry and gentle, innuendo-packed presenting style was a big part of the programme's success as it grew from an audience of two million on BBC Two to nearly 16 million at its peak on BBC One. But Anthony Bourdain, of course, had a no bullshit take on what was really going on here.

"Fans of our many TV chefs have come to believe that chefs are adorable, cuddly creatures in spotless white uniforms all too happy to give them a taste of what they're whipping up at the time. The truth is somewhat different. What's been lost in all this food-crazy, chef and restaurant-obsessed nonsense is that cooking is hard. . . and requires skills other than, and less telegenic than, spouting catchphrases and schmoozing." Whoah!

So, cooking has become something more than a matter of life and death and the ratings. Bourdain's *Kitchen Confidential* mystique has been shattered by cooks like . . . well, like Anthony Bourdain, and cookery producers like the *Great Bake Off* brain-dead dumbos. A working class hero *may well* be something to be (right on, John Lennon). But a celebrity chef is the bees knees *to be*, no ifs no buts. And remember, you heard it here first!

Back in 1987, we thought Café Josie's magic theme was the ultimate USP device from the *Forbidden Planet* coz we'd worked it all out so that nothing could go wrong. Yeah, right. But if Houdini feasted on the adulation triggered by his disappearing elephant trick, we didn't notice that he'd parked it in our diner. And neither did even the most unlikely of our paying customers. All were entranced by our theme tune.

I recall the time I was deep-cleaning the kitchen during a summer weekend and Mum was out front doing her bit with all the linen when she said a health inspector had arrived! I thought he was calling to make an unannounced inspection, but no. He said it was a routine call to warn us not to serve a certain commercial pate that had been recalled on health grounds. Of course, I assured him we always made our own, and invited him to inspect the kitchen.

He was pleasantly surprised and popped his head in for the most cursory of glances. He said he rarely ate out, largely because of what he'd seen in the course of his work as a public health official. But after looking at the menu and being told about the magic, he said he'd like to book a table for his family that Saturday. I had to disappoint him because by now, Saturdays were fully booked three weeks in advance. So, he settled for a Friday the following week, and he and his family became regulars after that.

I didn't let on, but I was so glad that the inspector hadn't called the day Kim and I were carrying out blue murder on the kitchen chopping board. It was a ghastly interlude I'll never forget. And also, the first and last time the Thermidorian Monster appeared on our Specials Board.

All the world's a stage

Especially when *Mercury Rising Meister* Shaun McCree (above) is at your table with wonders to behold . . . and when Rich with Roy Johnson (below left), a regular Saturday night guest, joined the fun at a Halloween , you had to blink. But when Harry Nicholls performed the oldest trick in the world, you had to blink twice

6 CAFÉ CONFIDENTIAL

Cooking for a living is about being part of subculture, a secret society . . . the joy of making something with your own hands is the purest way of giving pleasure (though oral sex has to be a close second).

ANTHONY BOURDAIN, 2009

TIME FOR A CONFESSION. For almost 20 years I've been conducting a secret love affair. This obsession would have remained untold had not the object of my desire decided to shuffle off this mortal coil stage left, so suddenly and without warning. Yep, dear Anthony himself is – or was – the man. Though I only fell in love 10 years after Café Josie closed. Which is why I was so shocked and saddened to hear of his sudden death.

At the time, this memoir was in the mix, i.e. being researched and thought about, when news broke in June 2018 of Bourdain's demise. He was, of course, way after Café Josie but I'd picked up his book when it came out in 2000 and as I rushed through his purple prose, I had a shock frisson 'what if' moment. What if he'd stopped by at our eatery? Such are the idle reveries that butter no parsnips.

But the time was out of joint and Anthony Bourdain never dropped by. He was still on the front line, living the nightmare of cooking for a living. He probably never dreamed he'd go over to the other side and join the new wave of chefs who were becoming part of the celebrity culture that today, in the 21st century, seems to absorb every activity that all human flesh is heir to.

Or maybe he did dream such dreams. Certainly, Café Josie was ahead of Bourdain's game, and counted among its cultural companions the denizens of the MADchester Universe. By the time we opened in 1987, the exploding cultural firmament of the 1980s was awash with the counter-cultural actors of every kind who, for a short time, would take over the world.

It was the time when MADchester spawned a host of TV newsreader superstars like Tony Wilson and Bob Greaves, a phalanx of world beating acid-house rock bands like The Smiths, Stone Roses, (Pioneers), New Order (co-owners with Tony Wilson's Factory Records), Happy Mondays, pop bands like Simply Red and many others too numerous to mention. And notorious night clubs like the Hacienda, which had a door-entry pass policy to die for (sometimes literally!)

This whole acid rock scene spawned the so-called Second Summer of Love which played itself out as the Death Star legend struck. The decade was an exploding Universe, scientists confirmed, having identified the galaxy's nasty little secret. It was the Death Star, they said, that did for the dinosaurs 65 million years ago. We even know its name, thanks to that bunch of maverick scientists at Berkeley's Caltech Institute.

Its name is Nemesis, the twin of our very own sun. And it swings by into our God-forsaken corner of the galaxy every 26 million years or so. It went like this, Nemesis comes flying into our galaxy, knocks over all those chunks of over-matter rock in the Oort Cloud, and sends one spinning towards good old Mother Earth. Cue mass extinction.

That was 26 million years ago and it's due to return any day now. So yeah, we were searching the dark skies for a tell-tale footprint, when Café Josie opened its doors. That's what I was feeling, and I was so grateful Nemesis didn't actually hit the week we went live. I think it's called pre-show nerves.

The hunt for the real Death Star began in the late 1980s and was co-terminus with the exploding MADchester Universe. The main unresolved issue was the status of that Universe. Was it steady, speeding up, or about to contract?

It was a scientific conundrum that Albert Einstein was familiar with. He had long wrestled with the problem as he tried to reconcile his two groundbreaking theories of general relativity and the quantum mechanics of special relativity.

And by the late 1980s, the prevailing view among scientists was that the Universe was slowing down due to the mutual gravitational pull of all its mass. Whoah! But if it didn't actually hit the week Café Josie opened, it made amends 684 days later. And Poof! Shazam! Talk about ultra-fresh *croque monsieur*!

So, there you have it, the secret of *how* Café Josie was able to disappear just like that – the mutual gravitational pull of its magical mass, i.e. its magicians! (That's what I've kept telling myself over the years. The *why*, you'll have to wait for until Chapter 12).

But before you jump off to end of the story, stay awhile or you'll miss a gory little nightmare tale of mine. It's a story which will apply to any other of you god-fearing folk out there thinking of going into the cooking business. And I blame it all on the Death Star.

Fact is, that when Nemesis wiped out all those dinosaurs on land, it left untouched many of the denizens of the very deep. That is, at the bottom of the oceans, where fearsome clawed creatures were living off carrion and other smaller examples of their species, like shrimps and prawns. Yep, we're talking about the crustacean commonly known a lobster, a scaly, hard-shelled survivor of just about anything the Cosmos could throw at it.

And not only that – it makes for an incredibly versatile and tasty meal for us homo sapiens. Not many dishes can claim to have survived the Death Star's best shot – and had their origins in a blood-soaked revolution. Step up to the cooking plate *Lobster Thermidor*! But why Thermidor . . . ?

Well, this cooked lobster dish was invented in 1890 by a Parisian restaurateur, and named after a popular play showing in theatres at the time. The name of the play *Thermidor* was based on the summer month of the French revolution's calendar which saw Robespierre's reign of terror aborted. Some even say the dish was tasted by Napoleon who came to power shortly after Robespierre's demise. (There is no record of what Josephine thought of this tasty morsel).

But whatever the colourful antecedents of this very singular Thermidor, there is an elephant in the kitchen when it comes to actually cooking a lobster. The one problem for us chefs is that the damn thing comes from the fish market still alive and kicking – so it's gotta be killed! And believe me, once you've been involved in this excruciating murder, you're not gonna want to be near one ever again. Like me!

Call me sentimental, which is what Kim must have thought as he talked me through the dastardly rigmarole. It all started innocently enough, as these things do. We were at the market and we were offered two huge crustaceans, fresh from the sea. They were still alive, for crissake, and had their claws tied up so they didn't bite off your arm!

Throughout our fish market visit Kim was absolutely unfazed, and back to Café Josie we went with two live, wriggling crustaceans wrapped in broadsheet newspapers, *The Daily Telegraph* as I recall. It had been one of our crack of dawn visits to the market for fish and vegetables which we made at least three times a week. Arriving back at the restaurant, Mum was already there, getting the linen ready for that evening.

I remember it all clearly, coming back, saying Hi! to Mum, with two live lobsters which we put on trays and covered with damp tea towels. Mum saw the wriggling and asked what on earth was under the cloths? I showed her, and she was mortified to see their claws bound with elastic bands, keeping them firmly closed. She immediately insisted we should remove them! I had to explain that it was for their own safety because they would attack each other – and maybe chop off our fingers, too.

I demonstrated by getting a pencil and picking up a lobster, I removed the rubber band from a claw and it immediately opened its claw. I basically let it snap the pencil in half! Mum got the message but thought it was cruel. "You're cooking them alive? You wouldn't harm a fly growing up, you loved all creatures!" Except wasps, I reminded her.

She was not amused and went off muttering to herself as she got on with her work. Mum was an excellent cleaner for us, house proud and recently retired after 25 years' service in the NHS. So, I knew her knowledge of the secret lives of crustaceans was somewhat limited, and let it go at that.

You, more informed readers, will know that lobsters are bottom-dwelling, nocturnal creatures that scavenge for dead animals, as well as eating live fish and small mollusks and other invertebrates of the deep sea. They have a rigid, segmented body covering hard shell exoskeleton. These creatures have eight legs; the first three pairs have pincers, with the foremost pair growing much larger than the others.

Lobsters have compound eyes on movable stalks, two pairs of long antennae, and several pairs of swimming legs on their elongated abdomen. Its tail is muscular like a flipper and used for swimming and propelling itself fast forward or backward.

As a huge pan of water boiled in a hellish cauldron of steam, I picked up the creature and dropped it in – with my head turned away. Hearing the hissing sounds and anguished squeaky noises upset me, even though I knew the thing wasn't actually screaming. Kim advised me that lobsters had no voice box, and the noise was the air escaping from inside the shell joints. But once that one was cooked, I said I would never do it again! After all, my job was starters and side plates.

We didn't have lobster every week, it depended on the market prices. Kim showed me how to tell if a lobster was fresh (even though they're all dying slowly when out of water). You pick it up, holding its body horizontally, and then quickly turn it over on to its back. It will immediately bring up its tail with a THWACK! to cover its soft abdomen. The quicker and louder it does this, the more alive it is. Well, my wannabe restaurateurs out there, has this put you off yet? No? Tread softly for what comes next.

If you thought that dropping defenceless creatures into a pot of boiling water still alive was blue murder, you ain't seen nothing yet. For then came the time Kim showed me another way of killing these great crustaceans that had survived the Death Star 65 million years ago. Talk about gory! It was enough to put me off ever serving lobster again. Which it did!

Are you ready for this? Just like Bourdain did in his photo on the cover of *Kitchen Confidential*, Kim always sported a favourite cooking knife slung round his whites. It had a long, sharp blade and was as dangerous as any pirate's cutlass. He whips it out saying "watch!" and places the blade between the back of the still wriggling lobster's head and thorax.

Then suddenly, he whacks the knife handle with the meat hammer. The hapless denizen of the deep died instantly, but the nerves all along its scaly legs carried on twitching. Whoah!

I was traumatised and decided that was it! So, much to Kim's chagrin, that was the last night we served lobster, and my decision was final. Yeah, you can call me sentimental. And there was another dish I refused to serve as well, veal. Most other restaurants have veal – calves' livers – as a speciality, but I wouldn't have it in the kitchen. In those days, calves were born and kept immobile in the dark, rendering their meat tender and light in colour. It was the sheer thought of all those wretched calves cooped up in factory farms suffering a short sunless life which appalled me.

On one occasion, Hedda came into the kitchen to say a customer wanted to know why we never had veal on the menu or Specials Board. I looked at Kim and he just shrugged and said I should be the one to explain. Kim would have had veal on the menu for sure. I went out to the lady and explained why. She demanded to speak to the owner and, fortunately, Richard was free at that moment. She went on and on about how you (Richard) could own an upmarket restaurant and be dictated to by a chef!

Richard smiled and said: "Well, the restaurant is called Café Josie and this is Josie." His arm waved towards me and he bowed and left me to it. At that, the customer became somewhat embarrassed, and I said I was sorry if I had confused her. She became calm and remarked on how good the actual menu was. I thanked her and went back into my domain. Kim thought it was funny, actually, so did I.

Which again raises Bourdain's rhetorical question as to why so many sensible, educated people so successful in other fields would want to give everything up and pump their hard-earned cash down a hole that, statistically at least, has proven to be a bottom-less pit of despair and mayhem.

"Wanting to own a restaurant can be a strange affliction. The chances of ever seeing a return on your investment are about one in five," warned Bourdain. "What insidious spongiform bacteria so riddles the brains of such men and women that they stand there on the tracks, watching the lights of the oncoming locomotive, knowing full well that it will eventually run them over?"

Bourdain confessed he didn't know the answer, but he would have recognised the mindset that overshadowed all of us as we tried to make sense of the licensing application imbroglio those first few weeks at Café Josie. It was truly a dispiriting, nervy time, a bit like a Ramsey *Kitchen Nightmare*, or a curtain call by Nemesis. The restaurant was as quiet as the giant graveyard across the road. Things looked bad! Hell yes, Gordon Ramsey!

And it was while the cooking magic was being firmed up in our kitchen that a new star of legerdemain was emerging out front among the serried ranks of diners who'd plumped for the Café Josie experience.

He was a young guy who'd impressed the conjuring community with his stage act and was now starting out as a close-up magician at Café Josie. His name was Shaun McCree, and the tables of Café Josie were his stage, especially for his mesmerising tour de force, the Mercury Card Rising.

But he never imagined that 30 years later, a slumbering zombie desperate to be brought back to life would capture his attention. And how it would revive memories of one of the greatest magicians of all time.

7 MERCURY RISING

Any reasonably competent legerdemain is indistinguishable from real magic.

FREELY ADAPTED FROM ARTHUR C. CLARKE, VISIONARY SCI-FI AUTHOR OF 2001

THE OPENING GUNS of Britain's colonial march to an empire on which the sun never set were fusillading out across South Africa's veldt at the Boers when the young, unknown vaudeville showman called Harry Houdini arrived by ocean liner from America for his inaugural tour of the United Kingdom in 1900.

Houdini's astute vaudeville agents had booked a Grand Tour of the UK that included shows in the capital and then out across the country. The huge popularity of UK music hall was astutely foreseen by the money-grubbing showbiz producers who had given Houdini his first break in fairground shows in hick, backroads America.

But it wasn't the King of Cards persona or the sleight-of-hand skills of a Man of Mystery that caught one canny producer's eye. It was the impossible escapology of the muscular young Hungarian immigrant Erich Weisz that had audiences in rapture.

So, the young Houdini had been advised to go to the home of music hall –England – by a shrewd Chicago impresario who spotted the potential in the young magician's escapology which wasn't making much dosh in America. Indeed, it was London that first played host to the unknown vaudeville artist, and from where he was to set in motion one of the most extraordinary pseudo-scientific collaborations – with the world's most popular author Sir Arthur Conan Doyle.

On his London sell-out debut show at the Alhambra Theatre, Leicester Square, the young Harry Houdini started as he meant to go on, brazenly challenging the forces of law and order to lock him up! From his theatrical lodgings in Keppel Street, Bloomsbury, Houdini set out to conquer the world with his keynote, master-stroke publicity strategy – the provocative challenge that no police cell could constrain him.

He duly bamboozled Scotland Yard's finest, escaping from regulation Metropolitan Police handcuffs with miraculous ease, and the new breed of sensation-hungry newspapers the tabloid press turned him in to an overnight sensation. The *Police Review* reported that Houdini's jailbreaking prowess had the entire "burgling fraternity of the country lost in envious admiration".

After his electrifying debut in the capital, the Houdini road show swanned north, taking in Birmingham, Stoke and Stafford, and thence into Lancashire playing to packed theatres en route to the North-west. And his grand tour included, of course, dates in Manchester and then on to towns in Lancashire including Blackburn and Burnley.

Music hall was big business and hugely popular as the age of Victoria's expanding empire gave way to the 20th century. And, of course, one of the young showman's celebrated bookings was at the Burnley Empire Theatre, where he dazzled audiences of almost 2,000 over seven nights of baffling escapology.

But everything didn't always go to plan on Houdini's first, groundbreaking tour. Certainly, he was not expecting the horror story that jumped on stage at the Blackburn Palace the week before he strode the boards in Burnley. A smart-assed audience member challenged him to escape from handcuffs he'd secretly doctored. Although he'd always prepared for such eventualities, the underhand stratagem almost beat the escapologist and he barely escaped in one piece.

The spectator who attempted to bamboozle Houdini was Blackburn author William Hope Hodgson who had brought along to the theatre his own handcuffs on which he'd plugged the locks.

"The illusionist had a standing £25 handcuffs challenge but suffered considerable injuries because of the doctored manacles brought by Hodgson, who later found fame as a horror story writer," reported the *Evening Telegraph*.

It's hard to imagine the atmosphere at the Burnley Empire all those years ago, for now the graceful building on Cow Lane is a silent, decaying hulk of its former glory. Which is why Café Josie is now basking in reflected glory as one of its signature magicians attempts to pull off the greatest trick of his career: to restore Burnley Empire to its former glory.

As the *Evening Telegraph* reported in 2019, Shaun McCree the close-up star magician at Café Josie, had been appointed a new director of the Burnley Empire Theatre Trust which is campaigning for the restoration and revival of this magnificent historic building, the last surviving Edwardian theatre in East Lancashire.

A great step forward in the campaign to restore the building was the award of £44,000 in Lottery funds in the final round of the Resilient Heritage grant scheme which will enable the project to move forward into Phase 2 of the restoration plan to establish the best way to achieve resurrection.

Burnley Empire, a hidden gem currently closed off to the public, was built for W. C. Horner of the Victoria Opera House in Burnley and designed by local architect G. B. Rawcliffe. When it opened in October 1894 with a variety show, it could originally seat 1,935 people. Among the many other famous names who appeared there were Charlie Chaplin and Dame Margot Fonteyn.

The review of the opening night at the "Burnley Empire Music Hall of Varieties", was a fulsome report of the wide range of variety acts that wildly enthused a full house of some 1,900 people. The review also paid tribute to Horner, and to Rawcliffe, "farm boy, cricketer, lifelong member of Burnley Mechanics Institute" and the theatre director who commissioned the theatre.

The review, word for word, ran as follows:

"The Empire theatre of Varieties, Burnley, was opened under very successful auspices on Monday evening, 29th of October 1894. there being a full house and judging from the continuous roars of laughter and the heartiness of the applause a large audience were highly delighted with the bill of fare prepared for their amusement by Mr. Horner.

Quite a galaxy of talent had been secured for the week and the programme is both lengthy and a varied one. Indeed, those who would grumble at the entertainment provided would be very hard to please. The inaugural ceremony was of the simplest possible description, the orchestra played the National Anthem, the occupants of the seats on the floor upstanding with uncovered heads, the audience signalising the raising of the curtain with an outburst of applause.

In its way, Monday evening's performance was a notable one, mostly because it marked a new epoch in the musical annals of the town, which has long felt the want of a place of amusement of this description. Miss Nellie Lovell had the honour of singing the first song in the new music hall, and she was very well received in her male impersonations.

Mr. F. Coyle, the comedian, had three turns, and was encored for the Monstrel Boys' Medley, *and he was followed by 'Catawheela,' a man in the guise of a cat, who performs all kinds of clever and novel feats on a bicycle. This item was also encored.*

The Sisters Paris won favour for their duets and dance, their vocalisation being excellent, but though they repeatedly bowed their acknowledgements, they did not respond to the encore.

O'Connor and Brady, the comedians and knockabouts, convulsed the audience with laughter by their business in which were some new and very comical features. They were so successful that the audience would not be denied. Barrello and Millay were very smart on the horizontal bars and provoked much laughter by their burlesque wrestling act.

Miss Jenny Valmore, the comedienne, who has achieved great success at the principal London halls, was accorded a very hearty reception and at once established herself a favourite, with A Nice Little Picture, eh? *While* Do You Want to Know What For? *went so well that the lady had to reappear, and gave* Wait Till I Meet You Outside *which was so vociferously applauded that another encore had to be acceded to,* What Do You Care? *being equally well received. But* So, You Went With a Bang *and was Miss Valmore's best contribution.*

Mr J. C. Rich, who possesses a capital voice, was heard to great advantage and contributed three excellent songs, The Footman *at once making him a favourite, and his encore song,* The Sheeny Man *being an especially good effort.*

The last item on the extensive Pilots of Greeters, which were very gracefully performed."

In 1911, the respected theatre architect Bertie Crewe reconstructed the auditorium with a new seating capacity of 2,100, and it is Crewe's auditorium that remains to this day despite several changes of use and dilapidation due serious neglect. In that same year, Crewe also completed the Shaftesbury Theatre in London and later, the Palace Theatre in Manchester.

Theatres Trust describe Crewe's redesign thus: "The auditorium is elaborately detailed with robust and richly formed plasterwork in the Classical style. As reconstructed by Crewe in 1911, it has two slightly curved wide and deep balconies, terminating in superimposed stage boxes framed between massive Corinthian columns supporting a deep cornice."

In December 2018, the friends group 'Burnley Empire Theatre Trust' (BETT) formed Burnley Empire Limited and took ownership of the theatre from the Duchy of Lancaster to save the building from auction and continue efforts towards restoration. BETT says it is committed to helping secure the building as an opportunity for training and educational and employment opportunities, as well as to facilitate a fully functioning performance venue for students at colleges.

It also aims to cater for private /corporate groups and professional and amateur theatre companies, providing them with a valuable performance space and adding a beautiful restored historic venue in East

Lancashire. So over to Shaun for the interim word on the state of play in mid 2020:

> *"It was recorded in Barrett's Directory of Burnley in 1945 as The Empire Theatre of Varieties and described as 'one of the prettiest theatres in the provinces, and replete with every modern appliance for the comfort of the 2,500 persons which it can seat'.*
>
> *"Burnley Empire Ltd is now Burnley Empire Trust, with four director trustees at the time of writing, and is now a registered charity. With the help and support of Theatres Trust and National Trust, a National Lottery Heritage Fund grant has enabled more comprehensive surveys and resilience projects to be undertaken and a revised Viability Study is nearing completion to outline the way forward for the Empire.*
>
> *"Since we began to campaign in 2015 for the Burnley Empire to be restored and saved from the*

> *Theatres at Risk Register, we have seen it as a journey – this is not a quick fix but an opportunity to involve people as an ongoing training project while restoring it to its rightful place as a feature venue for Burnley and East Lancs.*
>
> *"The Empire began as a state-of-the-art music hall which was the pride of the town. It was the first place to show moving pictures in Burnley in 1896 and was remodelled as a cinema in the 30s, before becoming the popular bingo hall fondly remembered by many residents until it finally closed its doors in 1995. It is now embarking upon the next phase of its history, being restored to its position as a venue for the community to enjoy its heritage and future."*

Thanks Sean. Chairman Sophie Gibson added: "The past 12 months have been really progressive as we've managed to carry out a large amount of work gaining much more knowledge of the building, thanks to the ongoing support from National Trust and Theatres Trust. The charitable status has taken months of work but of course all good things come to those who wait and there's a long exciting road ahead for us all."

BET Trustees had the opportunity to visit Stockport Plaza, a venue with a similar story which was saved by volunteers. It now proudly operates as an award-winning, restored Art Deco venue which has been featured in well-known TV productions such as *Peaky Blinders* and recently hosted the number one album launch for well-known Stockport band Blossoms.

But if the BETT campaign is going great guns, it still has some way to go before it makes the kind of impact Shaun's signature mystery had on Café Josie diners all those years ago. He called the trick Imagination and it involved a Mercury Rising folded playing card. So, I'll hand over to Rich to tell you how it went . . .

"Ok Jo, thanks. Shaun told his watching diners, it probably helps if you've had a drink or two, because what you're about to see does mess with your mind; you can suffer serious psychological damage, if we're not careful. This is how this trick goes...

Shaun shuffles and cuts a deck of cards and asks someone at the table to merely think of a playing card, as he riffles his finger down the edge of the pack. He holds a break at the card thought of, so everyone else can see it, while he turns his head away.

Then he squares up and shuffles the pack, and he fans the cards out toward the spectator who chose the thought of card. He then reaches into the fan and he mimes taking out a card which, of course, is imaginary and therefore no one can see, and hands it to the spectator.

Now, says Shaun, he's going to rely on the spectator's imagination, because he asks him to fold the imaginary card in half, then into quarters, "in a kind of mental origami". Shaun then cuts the deck and asks the spectator to place the invisible folded card on to the pack and complete the cut, burying the imaginary card in the deck.

He then reaches over to a nearby lady and asks for a long strand of her hair – which no one can see because it's imaginary! – which he wraps around the pack. He then

MERCURY RISING

asks the lady to pull on her invisible strand of hair. And as she does so, a folded card rises up out of the middle of the pack. Screams of nervous surprise greet this sight. Really!

Shaun plucks the card out of the air and proceeds to unfold it saying: "Now you just thought of a card you imagined you saw, you folded that card in half, then into quarters and then you put the card you thought of back in the pack, yes?" With the whole table watching in rapt attention, the spectator, of course agrees, somewhat disbelievingly.

As he speaks, Shaun slowly turns round the card he's unfolded revealing its face to the audience as the selected, merely thought of card. Cue close to mass hysteria, I kid you not! Shaun hailed this mystery as one of his all-time favourites, a trick that he specially developed at and for Café Josie.

For which we were most exceeding grateful, Your Honour.' And it was to the legal arena that Café Josie looked when our legendary magician Rovi came face-to-face with a real-life mobster who offered to trade oodles of dosh for a secret from the Welsh magician's legerdemain arsenal.

8 ZEN, BALDUCCI & THE FORCE

The story is told of an acolyte who fell to his knees before the feet of the Master to seek enlightenment in the dark arts, and was tongue tied by the myriad of questions he wanted ask. But the Master rasped him across the backside with his cane. The pupil cried out, "Master why did you strike me?" To which the Master replied: "IT does not need your questions."

FREELY ADAPTED FROM EUGENE BERGER, SOCIETY OF AMERICAN MAGICIANS, 1983

TRADITIONALLY, WHEN CHRISTMAS IS COMING and the goose is getting fat, you're always on the look-out for those special little extras among all the festive joy. And thanks to a legendary Halifax confectioner, we had some super tasty extras to die for. Individually wrapped sumptuous chocolates that are Mackintosh Quality Street, a bowl of which graced every table.

And if you don't expect turkeys to be joining the Christmas Carols chorus line, nor do you expect to have a live grenade lobbed into your bookings diary. But that's what happened our first Christmas as the good ship Café Josie got underway. It was the UK Press a'calling, and they wanted to party in style with everything they'd heard that Café Josie was wowing diners with.

It's difficult to overstate the depths of opprobrium into which the UK press has fallen in the public estimation. The crisis has been sharpened by the fall-out from the Leveson Inquiry into the underhanded methods of national newspapers and calls for statutory controls. But the much-heralded eve of Halloween shoot-out at the Privy Council Corral between the Fleet Street Gang and the Hacked Off Brothers failed to materialise. Cue grumblings for Leveson Phase 2.

With both sets of gunslingers refusing to blink first, and Federal Marshal Wyatt Leveson lying stumm in the long grass with his £5m blunderbuss of a report, the inquiry's elderly pensioner chairman must have wondered what all the fuss was about. He was only being asked to counter-sign Press freedom's death warrant! For the Queen was being asked to initial a Royal Charter which, the Fleet Street Gang said, would usher in the first state regulation of the Press since it was abolished in 1695.

The big issue which triggered the Leveson inquiry was the phone hacking scandal which has dominated the public discourse over the last two decades. Among the high-profile stories was the sexual proclivities of A-Lister Hugh Grant. The *Four Weddings and a Funeral* star was on a visit to Tinseltown in 1995. And while sitting in his white BMW convertible parked in the red-light district off Hollywood's Sunset Boulevard, he was caught in *flagrante delicto* sharing exotic sexual favours with a black hooker named Divine Brown.

The *News of the World* reportedly lured Miss Brown with £100,000 to tell all for a copyright story about the incident that left the actor well miffed. Hugh Grant's response was to call for the entire tabloid Press to be shut down. The Hacked Off pressure group said the *News of the World*'s eavesdropping dirty tricks had a far more sinister agenda. Nothing less than a covert attempt to control the political discourse through a systematic compilation of incriminating files on leading politicians and public figures.

So, it wasn't just the phone hacking for celebrity tittle-tattle that Grant called on Leveson to investigate. Grant told *The Independent*: "I want him to establish that intimidation of politicians by elements of the popular press – by keeping dossiers on their private lives – was effectively blackmail."

So far, only the *News of the World* has given up the ghost and shut down. The "Divine episode" has been tough for Grant to live down, but he hasn't given up. He still heads up the Hacked Off campaign, which has taken a more targeted approach on how to deal with media malfeasance. He insists that newspapers' defence of the "public interest" at the inquiry were spurious. And worse, the political class didn't seem to regard phone hacking as a priority.

Among other celebrities who claimed their phones were hacked were Sienna Miller, Abi Titmuss, Sheryl Gascoigne and Harry Potter author JK. Rowling. All were given "core participant" status by Leveson at the inquiry, where a leading libel lawyer argued that irresponsible interpretations of press freedom amounted merely to "the freedom to wreck lives" in the newspapers' obsession with celebrity.

Fleet Street's case hasn't been helped by the sensational *Sun* story that the Queen favoured Brexit! And for the first time, a royal complaint was filed in the name of the monarch with the Independent Press Standards Organisation. Meanwhile, the Press has been discomfited by public opinion on the issue. Most surveys have showed a large majority of people in favour of some sort of control over what the press can and can't print. Especially when it comes to intruding into private lives.

But, as one correspondent wrote to *The Independent,* the public have only themselves to blame. Newspapers only published what they knew people wanted to read. "Scandal sells, panders to a voracious, voyeuristic, gossip-addicted public. The Press feeds on a depraved appetite of a mass readership."

There is a profile definition of people who read newspapers, which some disinterested observers may find illuminating – for all the right reasons, of course. And it goes like this:

Readers of The Times think they run the country
Daily Mail readers think they should be running the country
Daily Telegraph readers think the country should run as it was 100 years ago
Guardian readers think the country should be run by Social Services
The Financial Times is read by people who own the country
Sun readers don't care who's running the country, so long as she's got big t*ts

As American gonzo journalist Hunter S. Thompson put it: "The Press is a gang of cruel faggots! Journalism is not a trade ... It's a cheap catch-all for f***offs and misfits – a false doorway to the backside of life." Or as Thompson's Mexican compadre El Pado put it: "Journalists are like vultures picking clean the skeletons of human frailty." (We still don't know how El Pado came to supply the gun with which Thompson blew his brains out.)

I know all this was in the last decade, and Café Josie was 20 years earlier. But can a leopard really change its spots? What kind of people were they who lobbed that pulled-ring grenade into the Café Josie bookings diary? Were they just another archetypal "gang of cruel faggots"? And what if I allowed a bunch of Fleet Street journos on to my hallowed ground? What would I – and my magicians – be letting ourselves in for if I accepted their Christmas party booking?

The party booking came from the Northern office of the *Daily Express* and *Sunday Express*, in Great Ancoats, Manchester, where journalists were hunkered down in a carbon copy of the black glass Lubyanka of the head office in Fleet Street. Beaverbrook

Newspapers had traditionally been Empire loyalists but became totally mired in Tory party propaganda when they sold out to Trafalgar House.

Rich assured me the *Express* party were "a civilised bunch of guys" – he knew them all and was their colleague on the sub-editors desk until only a few months ago. He thought they'd be no trouble. But I still had my doubts about whether any magician could handle them. Rich agreed and said it probably couldn't be just anyone, we needed a "card mechanic". But who?

Then I remembered we'd seen such a magi who was a dead ringer for the Hollywood hard man poker-player in *The Sting*. His name was Mick Chardo who we'd seen doing his stuff around tables when we'd dined out in Chinatown some months earlier. What struck us was Mick's Doyle Lonnegan demeanour adopted by Robert Shaw for the movie. Talk about a hard-bitten gambler's poker face! Mick might have been an understudy and just walked off the film set.

But for all that 10 tons of butter wouldn't have melted in his mouth, Mick's card tricks were nothing short of miraculous. We'd even booked him in for a spot once, even though we did worry how that hustling gambler's persona would go down with what we liked to think were Café Josie's refined diners. But the *Express* Christmas party? He'd be perfect, we needed him. So, Mick Chardo was booked.

It is uncertain whether the New York City civil engineer Edmund Mariano Balducci ever got down and dirty and was forced to confront the tsunami of effluent in the Big Apple's sewer tunnels. Cutting deeper beneath the city streets was not really his game, as far as we can tell. But he'd probably have recognised Hunter

S Thompson's characterisation of journalists as a breed fit only for the sewers. (Balducci, 1906-1988, died six months after Café Josie opened).

What Balducci left the conjuring fraternity was the modus operandi of two arcane mysteries – the great levitating man aka David Blaine, and an ever-present weapon in any magician's arsenal, the power of the "cut deeper force". It's strange how cultural actors in different fields often mirror each other. *First Cut is the Deepest* was a hit record for Cat Stevens in 1967, and subsequently covered by many other artists over the years including Rod Stewart.

The song is a symphonic counterpoint to any card shark's masterstroke of legerdemain. All magicians will know what's going on here. But most of these concepts are beyond my comprehension, so I'll leave Rich to describe the "encounter of the century" that unforgettable Friday night – unstoppable Press gang meets immoveable card mechanic.

Ok Jo, thanks. The Express *crowd numbering about 20, were in good cheer when they trooped in to take their seats, and I exchanged some boisterous banter with most of them. My former colleagues started as they meant to go on, and within minutes of ordering their pre-meal drinks, they were*

MERCURY RISING

*demanding I do a trick for them,
right then and there. Whoah!*

*Well, I can't say I was surprised,
and like a good member of Baden
Powell's brigade, I was prepared.
I knew it had to be short and
snappy, probably a card trick. So,
I smuggled in Roy Walton's killer
Card Warp (well known to all
magicians). It only took two
minutes and went down a storm.*

*To shouts of "more!" I waved my
hand in the direction of Mick
Chardo (whom I'd briefed) and
saying "nah" to more, I
announced "here's my guest magi
tonight who does real magic!" Cue
rowdy cheers, as I stepped back,
and Doyle Lonnegan sidles into
the jaws of death aka the middle of
the now raucous Express party
table.*

*I didn't know in advance what
Mick was going to do, but I was
secretly willing him on to blow my
former colleagues away. He didn't
let me down. Mick reaches into
his jacket pocket and pulls out a*

MERCURY RISING

small brown paper bag, and he tells the now hushed throng that he's been studying Egyptian archaeology, and has discovered the Eye of Horus with which magicians used to do tricks at the Giza pyramids. Cue guffaws of incredulity all round.

Mick reaches into the bag and pulls out a pack of cards, and offers the pack to the nearest diner, and asks him to cut the deck. He does so and is invited to thumb off five cards from the cut half of the deck and hand them round without letting Mick see the face of the cards. By now, there is a wolfishness in the atmosphere as the Express *pack anticipate that they're gonna nail Mick.*

Mick nods, never once allowing even the hint of a smile to crack that poker face. He picks up the paper bag and reaches in to pull out a glass eye, which, he announces in an extreme low-key manner, "is the Eye of Horus". Cue even more raucous guffaws of incredulity. Unfazed and without batting an eyelid, Mick drops the

Eye back in the paper bag and hands it to the nearest Express *party diner who he tells to drop in his card. The other four cards are also dropped in one by one, and Mick steps back.*

He asks the last person who dropped in a card to hold the bag high up so the whole table can see. Mick then puts a hand up to his forehead, shades his eyes, and reels off the value of all five cards one by one. For a moment, there is a split second of astonished silence. Then the party table is in an uproar of cheers and clapping. Mick nods, without batting an eyelid or loosening up an inch of his poker-faced expression.

Then, inevitably, comes the smart-assed intervention, spat out by one agitated diner who clearly doesn't like being taken for a ride aka being tricked by a conjuror. "You didn't let anyone shuffle the cards," he roars, to murmurs of approval all round. Mick nods, and as steely-faced as ever, asks the objector whether he can shuffle cards. "Ya, of course," comes the reply. Mick hands him the deck, and the Mr Mouthy makes a pig's ear of riffle-shuffling the cards.

"The reason you can't shuffle is that you didn't remove the jokers" Mick says as if he's the coroner pronouncing the cause of death at an inquest. Mick takes back the deck, looks through and removes two jokers. Then does a flawless faro shuffle, as the stunned table looks on totally mesmerised. He hands the deck to Mr Mouthy and asks him to cut off a third of the cards and turn them face up on to the pack. He then tells Mr Mouthy to cut deeper, about two thirds, and again turn the cut portion face up on to the pack.

Mick then instructs Mr Mouthy to ribbon spread the cards across the table cloth, remove the first five face-down cards and distribute them to his colleagues. He then reaches into the paper bag and removes the glass eye which he proceeds to roll along the ribbon spread cards on the table. As the eye comes to a halt, Mick reveals the values of all five cards in quick-time order. Cue a second outbreak of thunderous applause, cut short only by the arrival of the first course.

Well Mick, I whisper in his ear, that was without doubt a pièce de résistance! (And thank heaven for Si Stebbins and good old Mariano Balducci!)

Well, Rovi returned the next night, Saturday, and we tell him all about Mick Chardo and *Express* crowd. He smiles, and says he wished he could have seen Mick's act. That was Rovi, always friendly, a fellow conjuror without airs or graces. He could appreciate what other magicians were doing and was always supportive of anyone who asked for help.

Whenever Rovi performed it was a magical night. He was cheeky, especially with women, but could get away with it. His Welsh lilting voice and smile won over everyone who met him. But even that mischievous smile almost failed to save him the night a member of the Quality Street Gang popped in for a meal. It was a close-run thing, and only resolved by Rich's well-honed diplomacy. This is how it went . . .

One of our solicitor's colleagues had made the booking for a table for two. He wanted a quiet meal with a client with whom he wanted to discuss his case file, without any interruption. Well, no problem with that. No diner was ever forced to see a magician. Patrons were always asked, by Rich if he was in, or Hedda, whether they'd like to see some magic at their table.

This particular night, Rovi was our guest magi, and we'd advised him not to approach the legal eagle's table. Well, Rovi was going great guns on the other tables and after a while, the lawyer signals to Rich who goes over to see what's what. The solicitor says his client would like to see some of what the other diners were raving about. No problem, and Rovi is ushered over to their table. I was in the kitchen, of course, so I'll hand over to Rich . . .

"Ok, Jo. Yeah, it all looked so innocuous, that never in a million years would I have guessed what was going to happen. Rovi, smiling as impishly as ever, goes over and does his signature opening request for a spectator to pick a card. The diner is dressed in a smart, dark coloured suit that hugs a massive frame, which betokens someone who works out. So far so good – and not so far out to lunch.

Rovi has the selected card returned to the deck and gets the diner to shuffle the pack, which he does with considerable skill. Rovi compliments him on his dexterity with playing cards. He takes back the pack and looks through it. He looks at the diner and mischievously says, I think you beat me! He removes one card from the deck, back facing the diner, and says, I think this is probably your card, the seven of diamonds? The gangster shakes his head, and hisses, not a chance, no!

Rovi smiles and flashes the card's face toward the mark. Are you sure this isn't your card? Absolutely! says gangster man. Oh, says Rovi, hold out your hand. And he puts the card face down on the man's palm. Now put your other hand on top, would you, says Rovi. And as the man does so, Rovi asks, well what was your card? To which the man replies, ace of clubs. Take a look in your hand, says Rovi.

The man does so, and his faces freezes into an expression of tortured menace. Still holding the card on his palm, the man swiftly grabs Rovi's wrist with his other hand and says matter-of-factly:

> *"I'll give you a grand to show me how you did that!"*
>
> *I watched this scene as if it was in a movie, transfixed like a rabbit caught in the headlights of a car. Then I snapped out of it. I looked the lawyer straight in the eyes, and said that Rovi would be unable to reveal any secrets because of "Magic Circle rules", even for money. To his credit, the lawyer understood immediately and turned to his client and told him "let it go". At which Rovi got his hand back, and I my beating heart.*
>
> *When the pair got up to leave, I escorted them to the door, and was full of apologies that Rovi had been unable to reveal any secrets. The lawyer smiled and brushed it off as he pressed two £50 notes into my hand. That's for Rovi from my client – with his thanks!"*

And that was how the Chocolate Caramel Brownie – not say Coconut Eclair– crumbled when the Quality Street gang rolled up to partake of Café Josie's magical hospitality. It's hard to imagine that the founder of these exotic sweets, John Mackintosh, would have had any inkling of where his creations would eventually lead when he set up his factory in Halifax in 1890.

And it wasn't until 1936 that his son Harold adopted the name Quality Street, inspired by a play of the same name by J.M Barrie. (Who once famously asked the sci-fi author H.G.Wells: "It's all very well being able write books, but can you waggle your ears?")

It was Harold who brought such exquisite chocolates within the reach of working class families, by packaging items in separate wrappers and in low-cost, attractive boxes. Hitherto, only the wealthy had been able to partake of such delicacies made from exotic ingredients from around the world. Harold also introduced tins for his individually wrapped chocolate concoctions.

By using a tin, instead of a cardboard box, he ensured the aroma of chocolate burst out as soon as it was opened. And the tins featuring chocs with individual coloured wrappers made consuming its contents a noisy, vibrant experience for the whole family.

And during the economic hardship of the 1930s, the craving for comforting nostalgia was assuaged by the chocolates and the tins featuring two characters wearing Regency dress, Miss Sweetly and Major Quality, both characters in J.M. Barrie's play. (The brand was acquired by Nestle when they bought out Rowntree Mackintosh in 1988).

So, originally a chocolate treat only within the ambit of the seriously wealthy, Quality Street had by the mid-1980s become synonymous with Greater Manchester's rich and famous and the houses they lived in. A fact not lost on the criminal fraternity who realised that plundering such gaffs was a no-brainer.

So much so, that Greater Manchester Police were forced to set up a task force, led by a deputy chief constable, to chase down what was loosely designated the "Quality Street Gang". And that is how, a member of this notorious fraternity came to be supping at Café Josie – and end up being blown away by a Welsh card-wizard and sorcerer.

There would always be a buzz on the nights that Rovi was performing. And there'd be shrieks of delight from Hedda and the staff as he got out of the taxi from the station. The atmosphere was always upbeat on those magical nights.

Our daughter Danielle, then two years old, loved him. Rovi would spend time upstairs in the flat with her and Richard and I would prepare them a meal.

He would then change into his tuxedo and bow tie ready for the evening. He often did a cabaret spot at the end of the evening and I always made sure kitchen staff could go out and see him, with me included, of course.

And before he came down to do his magic, I would join them upstairs and massage Rovi's hands to loosen them up, as he put it. He had been in a terrible car accident some years before, and his grip around a deck of cards hadn't been the same since. That's all I can say about it. He appreciated all the attention, because it was given with great affection by us.

(Oh, dear, writing this memory is tinged with sadness as Rovi passed away in 1996. I can still hear his voice now . . . "are you thinking of a red card, diamond or a heart? . . . yours or mine?")
Rovi, Welsh card wizard from Caernarfon I miss you!

Of course, Houdini, the original King of Cards, had seen all such card tricks long before. But what really obsessed him during the last two years of his life, was the spiritualist movement's recourse to unearthly powers to explain any inexplicable phenomenon. And, as we shall see, he went to his grave on October 31 1926, still battling the crazy clairvoyants who had even the White House under their spell.

And yet, Houdini failed to foresee his own demise, though he knew perfectly well he was tempting fate. And in her seminal biography the *Life and Many Deaths of Harry Houdini*, Ruth Brandon makes a convincing case that Houdini pushed his endurance envelope to its extreme not only for theatrical effect, but because he had a morbid fixation caused by the death of his mother. And Brandon recounts many cases where the great man almost failed in his death-defying acts.

As Bharat Rao records in his book *Magical*, Houdini put it thus: "The easiest way to attract a crowd is to let it be known that at a given time and a given place, someone is going to attempt something that in the event of failure, will mean sudden death."

So, a word of warning to any readers of a nervous disposition – when science gets involved in bending Nature's laws, the result can seem, well, the stuff of the *X Files* or the supernatural. Science becomes magic – and how quantum mechanics upbraided the world's oldest trick is truly the stuff of nightmares.

As it was for the shocked diner who got caught up in its frightening entrails one Halloween. So you may want to negotiate the next chapter delicately in the interests of your sanity...

9 DEMONS AT HALLOWEEN

*Fear can give you an
extraordinary energy. Try to
turn it into its positive form:
theatrical excitement.*

YOSHI OIDA

Disclaimer: This is an unexpurgated account of proceedings at Café Josie during one fantastical night of Halloween. It needed no embellishing, no added detail to spice it up. This is catering and conjuring exactly how it was, in the raw, as Anthony Bourdain might have said.

THE STRANGLED HOWL OF TERROR was clearly heard in the kitchen and stopped the brigade dead in its tracks on a very busy night. It was a shriek which could have awakened the sheeted dead in their thousands across the road, and even the Great Houdini slumbering in his tomb in far away Queens, New York.

I rushed out from the kitchen to an amazing sight. The whole restaurant, every table, had stopped eating and hushed diners were peering over at a table in the centre of the room, where Rich stood looking nonplussed. The crockery and cutlery were scattered all over the table and in the midst of the mess was a smashed coffee mug in a thousand pieces.

It was the night of our Halloween Special, and the place was packed with diners, most in outlandish gothic horror garb. I sidled over to Rich and he enigmatically whispered: "It was the spider chop cup."

I looked at the shaken women diner who'd flung down the cup in terror, and I asked if she was all right. She nodded sullenly, recovering her poise, and the whole room resumed their meals.

I picked up the smashed cup pieces from the table and floor, cleared the mess away and smoothed down the tablecloth with a napkin. Rovi, who had been performing at the next table, looked at me quizzically and whispered in my ear as I returned to the kitchen, "that's the best chop cup I've seen", and resumed his turn at the tables.

The evening's proceedings resumed, including the Halloween cabaret also featuring Rovi, whose feats of mindreading, including the tossed-out deck trick, baffled everyone. Later, after all the diners had left, and staff — and Rovi — were enjoying a late meal, I asked Rich about his chop cup.

This is what he told me . . .

"A chop cup is the ultimate, stripped-down version of the world's oldest trick using just a single cup. The classic cups and balls trick figures in hieroglyphs on the pyramid walls at Giza. And down centuries across the world, there are accounts of street conjurors doing the trick.

The only magician we had at Café Josie who performed the authentic full three cups and balls was Harry Nicholls who learned his routine off one of the old masters of the Fifties, Ken Brooke.

Harry's routine was a joy to watch, right up close on the tabletop, all three cups within touching distance. Diners must have thought that he really was practising the dark arts as the balls moved around of their own volition, invisibly. This was true necromancy of a high order, and could have got Harry burned at the stake in another time, in another place. Superb!

The expressions on the faces of diners watching Harry were only equalled on a 13th-century Old Master painting by Hieronymus Bosch in his most famous picture, The Conjurer. *(I still owe Shaun McCree for the biscuit-coloured ceramic coffee mug he'd lent me which shattered that Halloween).*

The chop cup, of course, relies on a quantum mechanical phenomenon, examples of which are commonplace. You probably see them stuck on your fridge door every time you go to slake your thirst with a cool Budweiser. The chop cup was first popularised by Paul Daniels, who broke out of the workingmen's club circuit in the 1970s and on to TV fame with his one cup and one little white ball routine – which looked like necromancy.

I'd always wanted frame a trick which, it is claimed, was derived

*from the world's oldest. The chop
cup was the start. Then my
accidental discovery of humanity's
favourite phobia sealed the deal
for me. Arachnophobia affects
70% of the population, young or
old, male and female, educated
or not.*

*And I realised I had the ultimate
shock impact in the simplest of
tricks. After all, fear is at the
centre of many big stage illusions,
whether the magician is using live
tigers or defying death by being
sliced up by an enormous spinning
buzzsaw. In my case, the fear was
provoked by a realistic looking
plastic spider, that appeared
in the cup.*

*Indeed, Houdini traded on such
fear in many of his escapes. Many
an audience was known to have let
out strangled gasps of terror as
they waited for the Great Houdini
to make good his escape from a
straitjacket dangling from a
skyscraper window high above a
New York street. And there was
similar pent up fear among any*

> *audience who witnessed his escape from his Water Torture Cell.*
>
> *I believe the frisson of fear aroused by hidden danger is pure gold in any magician's arsenal. (And if your name is Harry Houdini, it's legend-making).*
>
> *Certainly, my formulation of the trick has stood me in good stead over the years since I perfected it at Café Josie. It's been the centrepiece of my spot whenever I've been asked to "do something" at a university function."*
>
> You can see how it looked at a recent Buckingham Uni Law Society dinner:
> *https://youtu.be/8HrCwWzl-Bc*

Halloween was always a special night at Café Josie. On this occasion, Richard had booked Shaun to head up the Secret Cabaret for the whole restaurant. We had the restaurant decorated for the occasion. I put on a black dress and a witch's hat at the end of service, for the Secret Cabaret.

I was at the bar when Shaun requested I assist him with his big special illusion. I protested slightly, then joined him. I lay on a table and he got out a ferociously toothed Black and Decker electric saw and sawed me in half! People were screaming as I "died".

You know, I don't think you could get away with that now! It was another successful evening for Café Josie. Halloween at Café Jose was always a night of surprises, colour, shock and magical mayhem.

So, maybe it is entirely fitting that on All Hallows Eve, one should remember the passing of the legend that was Harry Houdini. And recall that towards the end of a life of death-defying feats, he maintained a secret, obsessive interest in the ultimate question posed by the clairvoyants who dominated the cultural firmament in the wake the slaughter of the First World War.

It was one of the closest secrets known by only a few that the Great Houdini took to his grave – the promise to his faithful wife Bess that he'd make contact from beyond the grave, "that undiscovered country from whose bourn no traveller returns," if it were possible.

Indeed, that's precisely why members of the Society of American Magicians, of which he was once President, have met on this day each year for the past 100 years. Their hope is that Harry will make good on his pledge. And why, when Society members meet at the Great Houdini's graveside in Queens, New York every October 31, few even today, are able to resist a wry smile at the date, All Hallowes Eve.

Indeed, at the escapologist's funeral in New York in 1926, pallbearer Florenz Siegfeld (of Follies fame) is said to have remarked as the coffin was lowered into the grave watched by a glittering roll-call of 2,000 mourners from the stage, screen and vaudeville: "Suppose that he isn't in it?"

The irony would not have been lost on the Handcuff King. For his extraordinary death-bed pledge – the last, little known secret of an eventful life – has been the source of controversy ever since. As was his collaboration with Arthur Conan Doyle, creator of the world's greatest fictional detective, Sherlock Holmes. It was a pact that ended in acrimony and legal vitriol.

Today, Houdini has permanent special exhibition at the Magic Circle's dazzling HQ in Stephenson Way, Euston, and a faithful following whose legerdemain is strictly law-abiding. And yes, even today at Halloween, members of the world-famous magicians club honour the memory of the world's first celebrity supershowman at their London HQ.

Houdini's first overture to Conan Doyle came following his sell-out debut show at the Alhambra, Leicester Square, in a letter cheekily addressed to 221b Baker Street. Intent on cashing in on the popularity of the Sherlock Holmes stories, Houdini brazenly asked for the great detective's assistance in catching a "thief who was stealing his secrets". It was all nonsense, of course, and there is no record that Conan Doyle replied. But the tabloid Press loved it.

Many years later, a grief-stricken Conan Doyle remembered the upstart young showman, and struck up a friendship that resulted in their bizarre joint quest – for an answer to the ultimate question, is there life after death? And over the last few years of his life, Houdini collaborated with the celebrated author in an attempt to establish the truth of spiritualism's claims of life beyond the grave.

"No two people could have been more different," said Prof Edwin Dawes, official historian at the Magic

Circle. "Houdini, short, stocky, brash, self-taught, and Conan Doyle, tall, cultured and magisterial. But each saw in the other qualities they admired.

"Their common interest was in spiritualism and Lady Doyle's claims to be able to communicate with the dead through trance writing."

Conan Doyle was first introduced to Houdini in 1919 when the showman was appearing in Brighton. Houdini had by now refined his act to the point of mesmerising impossibilities. He did this usual shackle escapes, but what caught Conan Doyle's eye was Houdini's astonishing feat of walking through a wall and its locked door.

Backstage after the show, the author confronted Houdini and challenged him over the illusionist's modus operandi. But before Houdini could reply, Conan Doyle provided his own solution: Houdini could dematerialise himself in one place and reappear elsewhere at will. A flustered Houdini, somewhat in awe that the great author had honoured him by coming backstage, could only demur and say that Magic Circle rules prevented him from disclosing secrets. But he ruled out any spiritualistic explanation, much to Conan Doyle's irritation.

Soon afterwards, the magician and his wife were regular guests at the Doyles' home in Crowborough, Sussex and Lady Doyle marvelled to the point of fainting at some of Harry's sleight-of-hand during intimate displays of card magic on these occasions. What brought the two men together was personal bereavement – Houdini grieving for his mother who died in 1913, and Conan Doyle who lost both his son Kingsley and his wife's brother in the First World War.

The idea of communication beyond the grave fascinated Houdini. But, as a master magician, he could easily see through the thinly disguised chicanery of charlatan mediums whose tricks he himself often used in his act. Conan Doyle, however, had completely fallen under the spell of spiritualism – and he'd been among many eminent late Victorian figures to have been duped by photographs in 1917 of the Cottingley fairies, said to have been taken by two schoolgirls, Elsie Wright and her cousin Frances Griffiths.

The craze for psychic phenomena had been started in Victorian England by the notorious spirit medium Daniel Douglas Home whose ghostly table-rapping and feats of levitation split public opinion: Ruskin was said to have been desperate to meet him, but both Charles Dickens and the poet Robert Browning denounced the self-styled psychic as a devious charlatan.

In the last decade of the 19th century, Camden, north London drawing rooms had been enthralled by the feats of a celebrated medium Mrs Guppy. Sir Arthur, too, became convinced that she was able to transport herself some two miles, from Highbury to Bloomsbury by ethereal means alone. And faced with the bravura legerdemain of a master conjuror he ironically forgot the ultra-rational modus operandi of his own creation, Sherlock Holmes: when you discount everything that is impossible, what's left no matter how improbable, is likely to be the truth.

"Conan Doyle believed that many of Houdini's illusions depended on the escapologist's ability to 'dematerialise' himself," added Dr Dawes. "Such a belief was certainly bizarre in one so well-versed in the natural sciences. But, of course, Houdini found himself unable to disabuse the writer of this absurd explanation without exposing magicians' trade secrets."

Conan Doyle took Houdini's reticence as confirmation of his belief, and over more than two years, the two men corresponded about their findings while attending séances in Britain and America. Time and again, the author penned reports of how he'd been impressed by the spirit manifestations he'd witnessed. But Houdini remained unconvinced. Having joined a committee set up by the *Scientific American* magazine which was offering $5,000 for proof of psychic phenomena, Houdini could scarcely conceal his scorn for well educated people taken in by spiritualists.

In the spring of 1922, Conan Doyle was on an American lecture tour with his wife Jean who had become a medium herself. Their aim was to propagate the gospel of spiritualism. On a holiday break in Atlantic City, Sir Arthur invited the Houdinis for a weekend. Lady Doyle had suggested a séance after "feeling that she might have a message coming through from Houdini's dead mother".

The great showman reluctantly agreed. Houdini recorded the date, June 17, 1922 – and precisely what happened. The séance was conducted at the Doyles' hotel suite in the afternoon. "It turned out to be the breaking point between the two men," said Dr Dawes. "The blinds were drawn, but by Sir Arthur's own account, Houdini 'sat silent, looking grimmer and paler every moment'."

Lady Doyle apparently went into a trance and drew a sign of the cross on the page of a notepad. A 'spirit' message promised Houdini that "happiness beyond his dreams awaited him with his mother."

Houdini later noted: "Lady Doyle claimed that the spirit of my dear mother had control over her hand – but my mother could not write English". But the last straw for Houdini was the crosses.

"The Conan Doyles were Christians. But Houdini came from a devout Jewish family and his mother was, of course, also a Jew," added Dr Dawes. "Moreover, June 17 had been his mother's birthday, a fact the message failed to mention."

Houdini left the séance without a word, scarcely able to suppress his anger. Relations between the two men cooled, with Conan Doyle unable to understand Houdini's blank refusal to endorse the author's spiritualist activities. While Conan Doyle continued touring lecture halls speaking in favour of spiritualism, Houdini was often attending séances in disguise and debunking mediums across America with increasingly vitriolic derision and maximum publicity.

Houdini inevitably made enemies of many spiritualists. Some claimed to have foreseen his death – or even may, literally, have had a hand in it (as authors William Kalush and Larry Sloman suggested in their book, *The Secret Life of Houdini*).

And relations between Harry Houdini and Arthur Conan Doyle became so toxic that the great showman, the year before he died, began legal proceedings to sue the author for defamation.

Houdini-Doyle slander Suit, screamed the headlines. *Controversy over Spiritualistic Exposes of Handcuff King.* The newspaper story said Doyle had criticised Houdini for refusing to agree the *Scientific American*'s prize of $5,000 had been won by the notorious medium Margery during five seances attended by Houdini.

The Handcuff King insisted no psychic phenomena had been produced by Margery, and speaking from the stage of the Hippodrome in New York, he announced he was starting legal proceedings for slander against Conan Doyle. The author was "a menace to mankind" because he thought his reputation in the spiritualism field was as good as his ability at writing detective stories, thundered Houdini.

The Great Houdini's crusade against spiritualism was only cut short by his untimely death. It came after he'd refused to cancel a show – which included his famous Water Torture Cell illusion – despite suffering from a ruptured appendix sustained in a dressing incident two days earlier. He had to be smashed out of the Water Torture Cell and was rushed to hospital where he died at 1.26pm on October 31 – All Hallows Eve – 1926.

And so, to that final promise to his wife to open that elusive doorway to the next world – if he could. Bess, in turn, had promised her husband, that each year on Halloween she would stage a séance with close friends to give Harry the chance to get in touch.

The final attempt came in 1936. Billed as the "Final Houdini Séance" in front of 300 scientists, occultists, magicians and reporters, it was broadcast live worldwide from the top of a Hollywood skyscraper. One last time, Bess's plaintiff call went out: "Are you there, Houdini?" But it was the one trick even the great master magician couldn't pull off.

A tearful Bess finally admitted defeat. "My last hope is gone. I don't believe he can come back. Good night, Harry. It is finished." Little did she guess that the legend of the Great Houdini was only just beginning.

Helping work the magic with a smile

Front-of-house chief Maîtresse D' Hedda had a smile to melt the frostiest of hearts, while Rich's brother Paddy made light work of white tiling the whole kitchen on his own.

All smiles at Café Josie's last party nite

Josie's Mum & Dad's 40 wedding anniversary bash on 18th June 1989 was the last big party night at the restaurant; Dad Joe with brothers-in-law Uncle Ted (left) and Uncle Dave (far right)

10 NeoROMANTICA MAGICANA

All memoirs are false to any writer; we can always invent a better detail than the one we remember.

JOHN IRVING, AMERCAN AUTHOR

SCHOLARS, AGNOSTICS AND SCEPTICS have long been wrestling with the import of the poetic lines of the Renaissance French physician, astrologer and apothecary Michel de Nostredame, more widely known as Nostradamus.

His collection of quatrains, first published in 1555 as *The Prophecies*, are said to have predicted a panoply of future events including the rise of Napoleon and Hitler, the two world wars of the 20th century and the atomic bombing of Hiroshima and Nagasaki. Many acolytes have even suggested he predicted the end of the world – a date coterminous with the Mayan calendar's prophecy of the same event in 2012!

Now I'm not saying I missed it because I wasn't looking when it happened (blurgh!) And I'm definitely not suggesting that Nostradamus also dreamt up a quatrain foretelling the evanishment of Café Josie. (Although some say he did!) No, what I'm reflecting on is what I discovered when I tried to bring myself up to speed on conjuration and the dark arts of legerdemain for this memoir.

Of course, I would never have asked Rich to explain the secrets of his magicians' illusions, nor did I want to know. Really.

But in fielding the words of those magi who so graciously gave of their time to provide memories of their experiences at Café Josie, I felt I needed at least to be au fait with the effect if not modus operandi of the mysteries with which they entertained our diners. (After all, I couldn't see much from the kitchen).

So where better to look than in Rich's personal magic library of books and DVDs? They say that the reader of books lives a thousand lives, those who never read, live only one. But I never imagined the cornucopia of delights I was to find in a library dedicated to the dark arts.

Among a litany of titles I discovered was Reginald Scot's *Discoverie of Witchcraft*, Nicholas Remy's *Demonalatry*, *Malini and his Magi*c by Dai Vernon, Max Maven's *Book of Fortunetelling, Soothsaying & Divination*, and even *Rovi Reveals* by Lewis Ganson, among many others, and a host of DVDs by – among many others–

John Bannon, Chris Philpott, Oz Pearlman, Morgan Strebler, Karl Hein, Diamond Jim Tyler, Mark Elsdon and an absolute load of DVDs by Jay Sankey, et al.

There was one discovery in Rich's arcane X-Files which I found particularly fascinating, a biography of the prolific diarist Samuel Pepys and his chronicle on Nostradamus' greatest prediction – about his own death and burial. Pepys, of course, believed in accuracy and truth in all his diary entries which spanned nine years from 1660 to 1669.

He was a true writer of record before newspapers were invented in the UK. (*Acta Diurna* was the first newspaper published, in Rome in 59 BC by Julius Caesar. The first printed weekly newspaper was in Antwerp in 1605). So, what was this Nostradamus prophecy that came to pass?

Well, the first thing to note is that the time span between the prophecy and its actual realisation was more than 60 years, according to Pepys.

Quite good going for any clairvoyant! Even one who also dabbled in horoscopes, necromancy and good luck charms. So, what exactly did Nostradamus prophesise about his demise on the 2nd July, 1566 in Salon-de-Provence?

He is on record as having repeatedly rejected being considered a seer. "Although I have used the word prophet, I would not attribute to myself a title of such lofty sublimity or attribute to myself either the name or the role of a prophet," he said.

But even so, most of the quatrains deal with disasters such as plagues, earthquakes, wars, floods, invasions, murders, droughts, and battles – all undated, which gained Nostradamus a notorious reputation. But he dismissed the idea that his quatrains should be taken as predicting the future.

A **quatrain** is a poetic style consisting of four lines, which has appeared in a variety of verse traditions of ancient civilisations including, ancient India, Greece, and China. During Europe's Dark Ages this form was used in the Middle East and especially Iran, by poets like Omar Khayyam. His *Rubaiyat* was translated and transmuted by Edward Fitzgerald (1809-1883) into a multi-stanza poem of translucent beauty, viz, here are three quatrains from scores in the Rubaiyat:

Awake! for Morning in the Bowl of Night,
Has flung the Stone that puts the Stars to Flight.
And Lo! the Hunter of the East hath caught,
The Sultan's Turret in a Noose of Light.

Come fill the Cup, and in the Fire of Spring
The Winter Garment of Repentance fling:
The Bird of Time has but a little way
To Fly – and Lo! the Bird is on the Wing.

The Moving Finger writes; and having writ,
Moves on: nor all thy Piety nor Wit
Shall lure it back to cancel half a Line,
Nor all thy Tears wash out a Word of it.

(Transmuted by Edward FitzGerald,
via Prof Jerome H Buckley, Collier Books)

Most academics reject the idea that Nostradamus had any genuine supernatural prophetic abilities. They point out that his predictions were characteristically vague, meaning they could be applied to virtually anything at anytime, anywhere. As they do with the Apollo moon landing in 1969, the death of Princess Diana in 1997 and the devastating 9/11 attack on the New York World Trade Centre.

Arch-sceptics such as James Randi, who demolished the Uri Geller spoon-bending bandwagon, suggest that Nostradamus' prophecies were interpreted much later by supporters who filleted his quatrains, so the words were made to fit events that had already occurred or were so obviously imminent as to be inevitable, a process known as "retroactive clairvoyance".

Sceptics insist no Nostradamus quatrain has ever been shown to have predicted a specific event before it occurred, other than in vague, general terms that could apply to any eventuality. And certainly, no quatrain alluded to the phenomenon of spoon-bending, despite what Geller may have claimed.

Ok, game set and match! But many supporters counter-argue that Nostradamus did, in fact, predict the French Revolution and the Great Fire of London! And what are we to make of that death's casket prophecy which, the diarist Pepys records, did actually come true?

Well, according to Samuel Pepys, before his death Nostradamus made the townsfolk of Salon-de-Provence swear that his grave would never be disturbed after he was buried in the local Franciscan chapel in Salon. But 60 years later, his body was exhumed, and a brass plaque was found on his chest correctly stating the date and time when his grave would be opened and cursing the exhumers.

He was re-interred during the French Revolution in the Collégiale Saint-Laurent, where his tomb remains to this day. So, why am I telling you all this? Well, it has absolutely everything to do with the Pepys connection and Rich's book, the acclaimed biography, *Sam Pepys: The Unequalled Self* by Claire Tomalin.

As the *Guardian*'s lengthy review of Tomalin's book put it: "Sex, drink, plague, fire, music, marital conflict, the fall of kings, corruption and courage in public life, wars, navies, public executions, incarceration in the Tower: Samuel Pepys' life is full of irresistible material which Claire Tomalin seizes with both hands! Fast, vivid, accessible."

And Rich also grasped the volume with both hands, too. As any good master of the dark arts would. Flicking through Tomalin's pages I soon came across the single, small plain black envelope, no bigger than a playing card on page 228. And indeed, inside the envelope was a single playing card, charred as if it had been in a fire!

Also inside the book was a scribbled note by Rich saying Pepys reporting on the Great Fire of London, which he watched for almost five days, was the perfect framing story for modern magician Joshua Jay's brilliant card fantasy, *Inferno*. Whoah! I didn't need to know how it was done, but it went like this ...

Pepys was a very social animal, and often played cards with group of friends across the river from where he lived. He'd been due to call in for his latest round of cards when the fire broke out, halting everything. From the safety of the southside, Pepys watched buildings on the northside go up in flames, including his regular card-playing den.

Tomalin's narrative of the progress of the Great Fire, and Samuel Pepys' reaction is storytelling par excellence. The blaze began at 3am on a Sunday morning the 2nd of September 1666 in Pudding Lane in the premises of a baker who had failed to extinguish the fire under his oven.

Pepys was awakened by his wife, but initially thought nothing of the fire he saw from a bedroom window and went back to bed. He was roused again by his wife at seven and decided to walk down to the Tower and view the outbreak from high up. He soon realised there was much at stake and took a riverboat westwards under Tower Bridge.

Along the riverbank he saw houses in flames and people throwing their possessions into barges and lighters (river ferry boats) and even into the water. Some were so reluctant to leave their homes that they put off evacuating until the last moment.

Pepys also saw the pigeons fluttering above, behaving in a similar manner, hovering above their roosting spots until their feathers were singed by the smoke and flames. "It was the most vivid and telling observation," says Tomalin.

Pepys stayed on his boat here for more than an hour and deduced that the blaze was being fanned by a strong easterly wind and that the long dry summer had made everything particularly combustible. He instructed his boatman to take him to Whitehall where he went to the royal quarters, warning people about the fire as he went.

Few people were aware of the impending danger, but the king immediately sent for Pepys who told the monarch to order the blowing up of houses in the fire's path to stop it spreading.

This proved impossible. "This was Pepys key role in the Great Fire of London, as the first to inform the king and the giver of good advice," writes Tomalin.

The king sent Pepys to the Lord Mayor with instructions to have houses pulled down, and with the promise of soldiers to help carry out this command. Pepys set off towards the fire in a borrowed coach and then got out and walked eastwards along Watling Street. There, he saw crowds of refugees many with sick people on beds crowding towards Cannon Street to accost the Lord Mayor Sir Thomas Bludworth who was in a state of exhaustion as he tried to enforce the burn houses order on reluctant residents.

"Pepys walked on, 'fascinated by the strangeness of everything' says Claire Tomalin. "His description of the fire is one of the most famous set-pieces in the Diary, and deservedly so. Most of it was written on loose sheets of paper, quite literally in the heat of the moment, and only copied into the journal proper later, and it follows his experience hour by hour."

Pepys then walked through the City again as far as St. Paul's before taking to the water again. The King and his entourage were on the river in their barge and Pepys joined them on the way to summon a colonel in the City militia to command him to pull down more houses below the bridge. But it was too late. The wind was carrying the fire into the heart of the City.

"The air was hot and full of smoke and showers of 'firedrops', the wind blowing a hard as ever," writes Tomalin. "When they could endure no more of the heat, they steered for an ale house on Bankside, and sat there until dark and watched the City burning as far as they could see up the hill, 'a most horrid malicious bloody flame, not like the flame of an ordinary fire'.

There was terrible noise too, from the cracking sound of doomed houses and the sound of the flames roaring before the wind. Pepys felt the horror of it – 'it made me weep to see it' – but he was also intent on recording the spectacle. On Wednesday 5th of September, after another few hours trying to sleep on an office floor, Samuel Pepys was awoken at two in the morning and told that the fire was at the bottom of Seething Lane by All Hallows Church where he lived. He immediately decided to take the family to Woolwich to where they'd retreated during the plague.

On the Thursday morning Pepys witnessed some looting, but nothing serious he noted, just people helping themselves to sugar from bags and mixing it with beer. There was no one about in Whitehall, and Pepys managed to get himself a shave before heading off to Deptford to supervise his household goods which had been delivered there. The fire was now finally burning itself out.

The next morning, according to Tomalin's account, "Pepys made a melancholy survey of the landmarks of his life which had disappeared. St Paul's was gone and his school with it. Ludgate and a good part of Fleet Street were destroyed with St Bride's, the church in which he had been christened and had worshipped as a child and 'my father's house' in Salisbury Court."

Apart from Pepys' immediate and personal losses, all round him more than 400 acres and 400 streets had been reduced to smoking ruins. "The medieval City no longer existed". Summing up, Tomalin further writes: "The fire was a terrifying ordeal for all involved, and it left a legacy of fear, but it was very different from the Blitz of 1941 to which it is sometimes compared."

There had been a massive conflagration, many destroyed buildings, but fewer than 10 people were known to have died, and the fire lasted only a few days. True, there was financial loss for many, primarily booksellers, whose fate Pepys laments in his diary. But the Blitz it was not, said Tomalin.

In fact, the political aftermath of the fire was more alarming than the blaze itself, with many wild rumours of arson and dark accusations of treasonous plots by French Catholics, the Jesuits and even the Duke of York. A haul of daggers were said to have been found at "house owned by Papists", and there was even talk of plot to poison the king. In the furore, Parliament felt it had to act and in late September 1666, Catholics were told to leave the City.

In time, tempers and rumours cooled, of course, but never went away completely. In 1667 a book was published claiming to provide evidence of the foreign Popish plots. And the following year, in May 1668, a meteor seen in the sky was hailed as proof that the rest of the City would be torched by Papists, who would cut everyone's throats. Nostradamus could never have dreamt up anything so wild-eyed and fantastical.

All of which makes Pepys jottings about the French clairvoyant and a dead, gamblers-den card player seem well, small beer. Pepys confessed to his diary he was beside himself with worry, as he felt one of his best friends had perished in the conflagration. And so, it proved a few days later when an inquest was held into the deaths of several card players in the gambling den. Pepys attended the inquest and gave evidence about his friend who died in the fire.

The coroner said, there was precious little left of human remains by which any of the card players could be identified, but one hand was found charred but intact, with a signet ring on a finger. Pepys immediately recognised the ring as belonging to his friend. And, added the coroner, the hand was grasping a single playing card, which could not be prized loose from his fingers. Whoah!

Rich's note said that Joshua Jay's trick now had an infallibly brilliant resolution. Any spectator asked to burn all but one card in a pack of 52, now had a target to aim at – the value of the card in the dead man's hand!

And, of course, the denouement was when the performer of the trick opened the envelope, to reveal the card chosen to be saved by the spectator: it was the dead man's card, charred 'n' all. In spades – or diamonds, clubs or hearts! Whoah!

I got it, and so did Rich who said *Inferno* was now his go-to trick if asked to "do something" for a crowd of people at University. But I didn't know how in heaven's name he'd do that! "How are you gonna do that," I lisped to him. To which he said: "You wanna know for real?" And he whispered, "best equivoque on the planet!" Yeah, right, I thought, how silly of me to have missed that! (But all magicians know the Force is always with you!)

So, now that I have a working, if hazy knowledge of what was up some of our magicians' sleeves, I feel more comfortable about introducing them to you gentle if sceptical reader, in this book's freewheeling chapters. No secrets will be revealed, only the colourful strands of the lifetime's obsession that brought magicians to Café Josie in the first place.

And what a dazzling vision it is! A scintillating array of magicians who enthralled diners over those hazy, crazy days of the MADchester Universe. And as the months rolled on, there were plenty of special occasion nights for our conjurors to deploy their skills.

During that first year of opening, the Christmas period for the family became a whole new experience. I don't know how I'd managed all those years before, cooking Christmas dinner for over 25 people in my tiny kitchen at home. But now having a commercial kitchen, it was a different ball game. Family, friends and almost everyone came to the restaurant, including Hedda and her kids.

For the first time we had a great venue, great people, great menus as well as paying customers, all being constantly entertained by some outstanding magic. And for the first time in my life, I really enjoyed New Year's Eve. Then the seasons rolled on. And at Café Josie there were always special nights to be celebrated featuring the best magic in town provided as usual by our little team of miracle workers.

At about this time we signed up a new magician, and new waiting-on staff all students at Manchester Metropolitan School of Theatre. I'll always remember my first meeting with our new magician Peter Clifford. Rich had fielded his phone call and booked him in for an interview. I was in the kitchen still working on the menus with Kim. We were wrestling with our master formula of 'cook to order', which, if we weren't careful, was an ambition fraught with problems. It meant we needed a menu that would be instantly and wholly manageable for speedy cooking and instant service.

It was while Kim and I were settling our plate tectonics that Richard interrupted me to come and meet a new young magician. Well, I walked out front to see this tall, gangly guy in a pullover and jeans!

Which sort of floored me, being an old-fashioned kinda girl. My first thought was, why would someone turn up for an interview in jeans! Yes, you're right, that was a ridiculous thought indeed. (Sorry Peter!). Peter was a drama student at Manchester Met and was also a very good magician.

He was cheeky and funny, and Danielle dubbed him 'naughty Peter Clifford'; after that we all referred to him as 'naughty Peter'. He did a couple of tricks for Rich and, of course, was instantly hired!

Peter was added to our roster of magicians, as were two of his university colleagues Lee and Kate, who were booked as waiters-on. Like all students, they needed the money and they proved excellent. Lee used to park his 3-wheeler green car out front. He called it the 'green bean'. But he always moved it around the side of the building before service, to make way for paying diners.

We had parking out front for quite a few cars. Soon, diners with more expensive models used to vie for a good spot. One such customer I'll never forget — I'll call him G — used to park his Porsche right in the middle of the park so everyone would notice. But it wasn't so much the car that stuck in my memory as the "mobile phone" he'd carry!

Now you've got to remember, this was in an era when mobile phones as we know them today hadn't been invented: the whole concept was absolutely alien for us then. But that's what G called this huge brick of a contraption attached to what looked like a car battery. We were in awe at the time when he asked staff to plug it in at the bar, so that his babysitter could stay in touch.

It's difficult to overstate how incomprehensible the idea of a 'mobile' phone was at the that time. Phones were usually located in big red telephone boxes on the street or housed in high impact-resistant polymer on desktops with a rotary dial to ring numbers.

iPhones? That was science-fiction to us back then. But for G it was a killer attention getter, and he lapped it up. (I did use to wonder whether he used his 'mobile' when he booked a table).

February came around and, with it, St Valentine's Day, a time for all young lovers to book a special romantic dinner for two. Ours became known as the Valentines Masquerade, where diners were invited to don their most imaginative fancy dress with the Romeo and Juliet theme. We had a prize for the best fancy dress and Rich's local barber Ron Keeling, won it first. Ron would figure large in later years when he tipped Richard off about Charlie Mitten, Manchester United's unsung Penalty King. The result was Rich's biography, *Bogota Bandit* published in 1996.

It was about this time that another of our magicians made his curtain call. Dave Allen had been spotted at the Magic Aid Convention by Rich, and subsequently as one of the featured close-up performers at the Blackpool magicians convention.

Rich said Dave was a very slick operator and there was one trick he did that was always a crowd pleaser for our diners. So over to Rich again. . . .

"Yeah, thanks Jo. Name of the trick was Razored Deck, and it was an absolute killer. It went like this.

MERCURY RISING

Dave took out his boxed deck of cards had them shuffled and got a spectator to select one, and show it all around, but not to Dave.

The card was returned to the pack and put back in its box. Dave then explained that as a close-up magician he was introducing an element of danger associated with big stage illusions like sawing lady in half. He reaches into his wallet and pulls out a handful of old-fashioned razor blades. Small, thin and incredibly sharp.

Dave then opens up the boxed cards and slips one razor blade into the deck, explaining that it will drop down to where the selected card is and nail it. He hands the boxed deck to a spectator and gets them to shake the box, which causes a slight rattling sound, much to the onlooker's surprise.

Dave then asks the spectator to cup their hands, while he opens the box and proceeds to pour out the cards which have now all been cut into pieces. As the last pieces plop out, everyone can see there is one whole card left in the box. Dave tips it out face down where it is seen to have the razor blade stuck right through the card.

Gasps of surprise all round as Dave asks the spectator to name their card, and turns over the razored card to show that it's the selected card. Cue wild applause.'

That was the effect Dave Allen always performed for diners on the nights he was booked in at Café Josie. But let Dave speak for himself. "I'll always have fond memories of the packed and buzzing Saturday nights at the Café. The great camaraderie between magicians, receptive crowd and the solid hard work, support and love of magic from Josie and Richard combined into something special."

For Dave it had all started in 1987, the year Café Josie opened. He was learning magic as a hobby and an amateur member of the local Manchester magicians circle. "Through club connections I was offered a spot in a "Magic Aid Convention" charity show at the University." recalls Dave.

"This turned out to be my 'big break' into becoming semi-pro. It led to a short TV appearance, an invitation to appear at the 'world's largest magic convention' at Blackpool – and an approach from the soon-to-be owners of Café Josie! Within months, I took my first nervous steps into performing card and coin magic for the tables of Café Josie."

Dave Allen especially recalls that at the time there was a lot of interest in so-called "table-hopping", close-up magic performed in restaurants, especially in America. "It was a very creative period with authors and performers such as Michael Ammar publishing a lot of magic designed to be performed standing up at a table," added Dave. "Most of my material came from books by magicians from the USA such as John Mendoza, David Roth, Derek Dingle, Paul Harris, Daryl Martinez and Richard Kaufmann."

One such book contained the secret modification to any suit jacket which enabled a magician to vanish or switch small objects, recalled Dave. "Luckily my mother had great sewing skills. To this day she recalls with horror the countless times she had to take the scissors to one of my Italian or Japanese designer suits."

Another favourite trick of Dave's was the piece of card magic which wowed Penn and Teller on their show in 2016. "It was Paul Gertner's Unshuffled, and it's still a great piece of card magic and worth searching for on YouTube," said Dave Allen. Of course, there were many other tricks in Dave's armoury, and among them were Cascade by Roy Walton, Pandora by Eric Mason, Mendoza Matrix and the Most Difficult Card Trick in the World by John Mendoza, plus Coins Through the Table, and Coins Across versions adapted from David Roth, Derek Dingle and others. Not forgetting the Razored Deck by Michael Ammar.

"Standout memories from Café Josie have to include, of course, the Welsh Wizard, Rovi, one of the stars of the show who sadly died in 1996. Whenever people involved with the Café get together, they'll sooner or later start quoting Rovi's jokes and lines," recalled Dave.

Shaun McCree also has vivid memories of Rovi. "I remember his classic lines (I think we all do!) And how simple his stand-up set was," said Shaun. "I recall him showing me a spectator cuts the aces routine that I think he had published, where the spectator turned the cards over to find they were all aces!"

The trick was given a fulsome description in Lewis Ganson's book in which the author recalls taking the part of the spectator during filming of the trick performed by Rovi. "At the time, it completely defeated me," writes Ganson. "And although I was able to see the film on several occasions, and piece together several clues, it was not until we recorded this [the book] that all the pieces fell into place."

The trick is simplicity itself, and so is the method, says Ganson. A spectator selects a card which is put back in the deck. The pack is cut by the spectator who is asked if his selection was a joker. Told no, the magi discards the joker and deals the next four cards at the cut, face down on the table. The cards are turned over to reveal the four aces! Finally, the pack is ribbon spread across the table – to reveal the spectators card face up in the middle of the spread.

Shaun recalls: Once, after Rovi had performed the trick, "he just ignored the spectator as he turned to me and said, 'now that's how it's supposed to look...'". He said the Welsh wizard was a massive influence, and getting to see him work regularly, was an education. "I remember the time we did a big Jewish charity function in town and the after-dinner speaker was Uri Geller," recalled Shaun.

"When Geller found out that magicians were working the event, he went ballistic and refused to perform if we were still in the building ... until he found out one of them was Rovi – then suddenly everything was fine!"

Rovi was held in such high regard by magicians everywhere that Shaun recalls how a special Rovi Award for close-up magic was smuggled into the trophy retinue of the British Ring of the International Brotherhood of Magicians (IBM).

"Few people know that we had to blag it because the powers-that-be didn't want another award, least of all one specifically for card tricks, even though Rovi was a past president," recalled Shaun.

"So, I arranged with Mike Gancia who was organising the competition that we would get it made and just have it awarded anyway, and once it was there it was hard for them to go back on it - I think Rovi would have approved!"

And diners certainly approved of Arthur Day, another magician who regularly graced the tables at Café Josie. Arthur was a master of Origami, the Japanese art of paper-holding. In one of his flexible creations, Arthur managed to get an Origami cat and dog at each other's throats in a shower of sparks – to the shocked delight of diners.

"Arthur's superb origami sticks in my mind too, the letters he sent were in themselves works of art," recalled Shaun. "People used to love the folded banknote shirts and the dog who moved his head to follow the cut-out bone in a little plastic sleeve."

Over the years, customers of Café Josie would go on to book many of Café's magicians for their private or corporate functions. "There was a definite blur between the magicians and the guests over the years, I think," said Shaun. "For some of us to have kept in touch with them - that probably speaks volumes about the unique atmosphere Café Josie had. I realise now, of course, we probably had a really quality team of regular magicians, as well as some great guest performers.

"There's little doubt that Dave Jones, Peter Clifford, Dave Smith, Dave Allen, Damian Surr and myself would never have found ourselves working together as often – or indeed at all – I'm pretty certain that we have all ended up performing at conventions and releasing material to the fraternity as a consequence."

Summertime arrived and we decided to close for the month of August. I needed a break, needed to spend time with Danielle. It gave me an opportunity to deep clean the kitchen too, even though we always cleaned down at the end of every service, of course. My kitchen was immaculate.

But just before we closed, the BBC paid us a call. And it was via the old, mid-Eighties phone technology that Café Josie scored a memorable coup when Radio Manchester phoned one day to ask if any magician could do a trick down the phone lines.

Luckily, Peter Clifford was on hand to work his legerdemain, as we shall see.

Stars of a Halloween party night to die for

Bewitching Josie, and (below) Manchester Met drama students Kate Hunt and Peter Clifford

Dracula personified is master of the dark arts Dave Allen supping a glass of champagne and blood, shaken not stirred

11 LEGENDS OF LEGERDEMAIN

*We are but shadows who come and
go, around a sun-lit lantern that
casts our phantom figures in a
Master's magic show.*

FROM THE *RUBAIYAT* OF OMAR KHAYYAM

WHICHEVER WAY YOU STACK IT UP, HOLLYWOOD has long been trying to catch up with the Café Josie Experience. How else to explain films like *Bad Timing*, *Memento*, *The Matrix* and of course, *Total Recall*. All these Tinseltown outpourings relied on a theme framed around fractured dreams and elusive, but persistent memories.

Memories are elusive constructs of the human brain which have long baffled neuroscientists and psychologists trying to explain their existence. They come and they go, like ghosts, unfathomable, evanescent and immaterial, spectres that shape our desires and our own individual version of reality. And they haunt our dreams, during those hours of unconsciousness called sleep, whose function is also still a matter of conjecture.

And now the end is near for this fractured narrative, it is worth reflecting on the how the screenwriters' construct differed from the reality of the Café Josie phenomenon. The writers' creations all relied on the imagination; the Café Josie experience counted only on real-life happenings. So, if this memoir has seemed impressionistic and jumpy, it's because that's only way I've been able to corral and capture those fleeting moments for this story.

What makes it all the more strange, is that many who shared moments to remember with us have only the haziest of recollections about the dreamscape experience that died. And it was 20 years later that I met one such person, while working as a therapist at a cancer support centre. He is a lovely soul – I'll call Morgan Stanley – who was obviously a refugee from the MADchester Eighties, given his predilection for having Bon Jovi blasting out as we worked.

The decade was studded with a phalanx of wildly successful new wave Manchester rock bands who were equalled by few others during that brief shining hour. But one group that was flying as high was the American hard rock outfit Bon Jovi out of New York. In 1986, their third album *Slippery When Wet*, sold 20 million copies worldwide. So, like memories, so like many energising dreams.

Then, one day as we finished our shift, Morgan mentioned some magic that he had seen on TV recently. And he recalled that he used to go with his wife and kids to a restaurant in Chorlton-cum-Hardy, when the kids were young. "It was brilliant, then it just disappeared!" he said, scratching his head. But he just couldn't remember the name of the restaurant!

Well, I rarely met the diners back in the day, I was always in our kitchen, in the thick of it. And suddenly here 20 years later, was a man who was so excited to talk about his family's experiences at the restaurant. About how good the food was, and how wonderful the magic! So, of course, I had to help him out, and told him the restaurant was called Café Josie.

"That's it!" he exclaimed. "And I still don't know what happened to it or Josie." That's when I let slip: well, you are looking at her! "What!," he exclaimed. "Yes, I said, I am Josie." (Cue the *William Tell Overture* as the Lone Kitchen Ranger rides in – Hi Ho Silver!)

I was chuffed to bits! It felt good to get such an excellent review 20 years after the booking, but that's how good we were. He was flabbergasted. He wanted to know why we just stopped.

He said it was always so hard to get a table on a Saturday evening. Obviously, we were very successful. His memories of Café Josie just proved it.

Well, we sat down, and I explained how the elephant in the room, sealed our fate. How, we couldn't turn tables, as people spent the whole evening with us, even after they had finished eating, all because of the magic. We just couldn't survive on just one fully booked night a week. It all might have turned out differently if we could have had a lot more sittings throughout the week.

It was a thread that even the Press picked up on when they called in to cover the appearance of another great American showman – from Georgia. Dan Garrett was a last-minute booking to do a guest spot during his tour of the UK. And his act mesmerised diners and journalists alike.

Dan had done the Magic Circle in London and was heading North, on his way to Liverpool's local magic club when Rich hooked up with his UK contacts, to ask if he'd like to take in Café Josie on the way, accommodation provided. For Dan, it was a no brainer, and proved a blockbuster. Diners were blown away and the Press went ecstatic, with pictures as well as reviews.

Part of the reason for Dan Garrett's success was his superb stand-up spot in our Secret Cabaret, which we put on whenever there was a magician willing to take on the late evening interlude. Shaun McCree was our booked magi, and he was well impressed. "Dan Garrett will stick in my memory, both for his stand-up and his handling of the linking pins, the first time I'd seen the Van Senus pins used like this," recalled Shaun.

Among the other highlights in Dan Garrett's cabaret spot were his Faustus Ring on string routine, and a very neat version of Cardiographic. It had our late-night crowd clapping thunderously.

Dan said of the Faustus ring routine: "Over the years this has become one of my favourite close-up effects. It has gained me recognition worldwide."

But the big revelation in the Press coverage was that diners who booked a table "were good for a whole night out". As a review by *The South Manchester Reporter* noted, we did not book two sittings, "so the table was yours for the evening" although, of course, the main focus of the review was really about Dan Garrett "from Atlanta, Georgia, USA".

We had stories in the *Reporter* on several occasions, once when Dave Allen did pyrotechnics at a table and a photo appeared with Richard and Dave. But the grey shadow forebodings in the Dan Garrett *Reporter* review were clear.

The *Manchester Evening News* also came down for Dan Garrett with a photographer, and they published a picture of Dan doing close-up and another of me and Dan as a rabbit appears in a saucepan (I know, I know). It made good press coverage and a couple of excellent reviews for us.

But there was still that elephant in the room, and there's the rub. We were booked up three weeks ahead for a Saturday but quiet during the week. We decided to try a Sunday lunch opening, offering traditional roasts. We put on chicken livers flambeed in brandy served on a bed of lettuce with homemade mayo, as a starter. I loved it and it was a hit with the diners.

However, the move was only partially successful, we could not fill the restaurant on a Sunday lunch. We tried lunchtimes during the week, serving a selection of quick cooked pasta dishes, such as fresh salmon in a lemon cream sauce; pepperoni in a spicy Italian tomato sauce; spring vegetables in a green pesto sauce. But the numbers were not there. There were no offices anywhere near from where we might have drawn lunchtime trade. (Location, location, location!)

But our dreamscape project rolled on, almost unstoppable. And our Secret Cabaret featured illusions you'd never have thought possible in a restaurant. Not only that, Café Josie soon became a focal meeting point for magicians from all over the country. "I think by then pretty much anybody who was working in town on a gig would call by after they'd finished, it sort of became an unofficial club house," recalled Shaun.

"We did share a lot of info with each other and lent out books and video tapes – back then when the VHS tapes were so expensive it was pretty much the only way many of us got to see the state-of-the-art material. We got to see people do a lot of other stuff too."

Like Dave Strange's Sword Suspension illusion, with Dave a menacing figure complete with black shades, which I could hardly believe was taking place. You wouldn't have either – if you saw someone suspended three feet off the ground just on the points of two enormous scimitars! Strange or what?

David recalls that ever since being bitten by the magic bug at 15, he'd been "determined to inflict my skills on members of the public, willing or not!" And he insists he was only looking to become a mere bit-part player in the Café Josie adventure when he called up Rich to arrange an interview.

At the time, David was working as a printer in a North Wales factory when, he confesses, he "somehow wangled" a part-time gig at the old Granada Studios Tours in Manchester, which hosted corporate events by night. "It was there I met Peter Clifford, who was establishing a career as an actor, but also a highly-skilled magician. He told me about a mysterious, wonderful-sounding magic-themed restaurant where he performed for the glitterati of Manchester society."

Peter Clifford shared the info that Café Josie was on the look-out for new magicians to add to their roster, and would Dave be interested in having his number passed on? "Would I? You bet your sweet ass baby! A week or so later, I was called by a suave and sophisticated gentleman who asked me to call in for a chat." Whoah!

Recalls Dave: "I remember it being a weekday evening and it was an hour's drive from work to my Wirral flat (on Merseyside), leaving me just time for a quick change, then another hour up the M56 to Manchester. I did a few embarrassingly basic tricks for Richard, Josie and a handful of bemused diners. Either Richard spotted my blooming potential, or he was desperately short of talent but either way, I was soon part of the front-of-house entertainment!

"I have happy memories of those days. Meeting other magicians, developing skills and eating some amazing food. Magicians were always invited to stay for a meal with the staff at the end of the night. The head chef Kim had a bit of a cheffy reputation, but his cooking was sublime."

The big problem for Dave Strange (aka David Smith), as he recalls, was that the travelling between Manchester and Merseyside left him permanently exhausted. He would not get home until after midnight, and then have to be up early for "my hated daytime job in North Wales starting at 8am". But the other drawback was the realisation that his technical skills, left a lot to be desired.

"I had taught myself magic from books and had a fairly high opinion of my own talents," recalls Dave. "This suffered a bit of a blow when I realised that some of the other guys were miles ahead of me. I remember David Jones showing me some magic with coins and it dawning on me that I had a bit of catching up to do. Of course, this is the best way to learn and those times were inspiring and educational.

"One of my favourite tricks involved making a borrowed ring disappear and then re-appear in a flash of fire. I had learned it from a book by a well-known magician called Wayne Dobson who was a sometime TV rival of Paul Daniels. Unfortunately, I was not the only person who had read that book. My friend Shaun McCree had made it a part of his act and I realised that I would have to increase my repertoire so as not to clash with the same material."

But the magician that all other magicians deferred to was Café Josie's one and only Welsh wizard Rovi. "I will never forget the legendary Rovi, a larger-than-life character, with whom I remember swapping ideas and sleight-of-hand moves at the end of the evening," recalls Dave.

"On one occasion, I'd recently learned a trick involving playing cards mysteriously travelling to a spectator's pocket or other seemingly impossible location. The trick had been published in a book by Paul Harris, an American magician, and Rovi seemed rather impressed.

"However, he must have mistakenly thought that I had invented the trick myself. A few months later I recall seeing him giving a lecture to members of a magic club where magicians had paid to learn the secrets of the master. He performed the card routine that I had shown him and was passing it off as his own invention! A magical rascal for sure! He will be sorely missed!"

Of course, even jesting that Rovi was some sort of scallywag would be doing him a rank injustice, for nothing could have been further from the truth. Rovi was nothing if not a gentleman and brought up to respect and fear the Good Lord, by loving, fiercely religious parents. They regarded a pack of cards as the devil's work, and as a young boy Rovi always had hide away his practice sessions, as he told Lewis Ganson for his book, *Rovi Reveals*.

As a result, Rovi became something of loner, after being bitten by the magic bug at 14. His one pack of cards was always in his hands in secret, "the devil's tools" – as his parents dubbed them – which he had to keep away from their praying eyes. He met a few other magicians in Bangor, but it was the TV mentalist Al Koran who changed his whole way of thinking about the magic art, he told Ganson.

Koran convinced Rovi to specialise in card plots that were simple, direct and easy to understand. Audience impact was everything, advised Koran, rather than any long-winded legerdemain. Displays of clever sleight-of-hand were trumped every time by inexplicable, fast effects that were simple, direct and therefore doubly entertaining. "Anyone who saw Rovi perform – as I did on many memorable occasions – knows that he took this advice to heart, and built a reputation known the world over," recalled Dave Strange. "When I look back at his many miracles with a simple pack of cards, I am still spellbound by the wonder of it all."

And bewildered, too, was BBC Radio Manchester when its outside broadcast unit called in at short notice to investigate inexplicable happenings at a local restaurant called . . . Café Josie.

They'd heard "via Chinese whispers" that diners were being given all manner of indigestion by "conjurors hopping on to their tables". Whoah!

Well, I'd fielded the call that sunny afternoon, when the Beeb asked to record live whatever it was that was so perplexing our paying customers. I told them, of course, it was our "table-hopping" magicians – and then almost bit my tongue. I didn't have a magician within a 100 miles of the Café at 3.30 in the afternoon. But, of course, I told them to send the reporter. What time could I expect him? He'll be with you in 15 minutes, came the droll reply.

Chinese whispers indeed! Han Ping Chien, a Vaudeville-era contemporary of Houdini, would have laughed his pigtail off at that – had he not been dead for over 100 years! Which I didn't know at the time, but later discovered when I gave our man at Manchester Met Peter Clifford a ring and begged him to come on down asap and rescue me!

Peter trolls up three minutes before the BBC outside broadcast unit arrives, just enough time for me to tell him what he's getting into – a live interview and a live broadcast demonstration of the kind of micro-trickery their "Chinese whispers" had told them about. I was close to having kittens but, fortunately, Peter was as magisterially composed as he'd ever been. And Kim had emerged from prep in the kitchen to watch this episode of "fear and loathing in Chorlton-cum-Hardy". Watch, not take part, he said.

"Jo was great and spoke articulately with passion," recalled Peter. "She extolled the Café Josie dream made real by her and Richard, the magic, the fantastic food and how amazing was her chef Kim (whose chest puffed up a little at the glowing mention). Jo even got in her pride at being a lassie from the North . . . especially Manchester."

Well, I was now really on edge, as I wondered how on earth Peter was going to bamboozle a hard-bitten radio reporter who was recording his every move. So did Peter, though he didn't bat an eyelid, as he asked the reporter if he had any small change in his pocket. The reporter reached into his jacket pocket and pulled out a handful of coins. "This enough," he said?

Peter nodded and the reporter clicked on his mike-recorder, and we heard the studio presenter say that they'd be going live after the record playing on air ended. Then, 3-2 -1, "Now we're going live to our man at Café Josie". Peter picked up four coins from the pile on the tablecloth and, paying homage to a Chinese magician called Han Ping Chien, proceeded to pass all four coins, one by one, through the table top into his waiting hand underneath.

It took less than 20 seconds, and it was all over. The reporter handed back to the studio, with the presenter saying the magic sounded great. "And was the food quite so special?" he asked. "Oh yes, very," said the reporter. I breathed a sigh of relief. I couldn't believe what I'd just seen, but whoah! Peter you're a diamond!

Peter recalls: "I'd chosen the coins trick because they would make a noise and I usually got good reactions with it from Café Josie diners. So, I was hoping that if the coins could be heard, it might get some of the magic across the airwaves! . . . Also, it was short. It seemed to go well; the reporter was impressed but didn't react strongly. But then, he had a lot going on for him too.

"I can't really recall exactly how it all went . . . so much was going on in my head that my brain had obviously decided to focus on the broadcast segment... But I do remember saying that people should come to restaurant to see all the fantastic magic and taste the amazing food for themselves!"

Well, our "naughty Peter Clifford" had come through for Café Josie again! I was over the moon, a Chinese moon. And that was a loose end I desperately wanted tying up. Han Ping Chien? Who TF was that? After the BBC crew had departed, I took Peter to one side and asked him to explain. No secrets, just explain. This is what he told me. . .

"Yeah, Han really was a real Chinese magician who toured America in the first decades of the 20th century with his family-based Peking Mysteries Troupe. He was born in 1891, and got into magic as a child, perfecting an act with tricks like multiple silk productions, appearing Chinese parasols and the production of multiple water bowls – not just one, but several tall stacks, all brimming full of water.

"He travelled all over the Europe and the United States at one time or another and died at the young age of only 39. But not before he had developed and perfected the sleight-of-hand coin magic move that bears his name, and which today is a staple among magicians the world over. Han Ping Chien, we salute you." Thanks, Peter.

So, what would Han Ping Chien have made of the grey shadow on the wall at the Café? As I look back and reflect on the fantasy project that was Café Josie, I am struck by our sheer foolishness and folly in not taking note of the elephant in the room.

As a result, like the original inhabitants of the Empire of Liberty, we refused to see the express train called oblivion speeding down the track . . .

12 KITCHEN IMPOSSIBLE

*Come the rolling thunder,
but first the flash.*

COMANCHE GREAT PLAINS INDIAN
WEATHER FORECAST, TRAD.

THERE IS NO EVIDENCE IN THE FOSSIL RECORD, chiefly the Burgess Shale, that giant pachyderms padded over the vast central grasslands of the North American tectonic plate around the time history's first mass ethnic cleansing took place. Their counterpart cousins the gigantic mammoth, were wiped out 11,000 years earlier by the species with whom they shared the plains, home sapiens.

Victims of that first ethnic jacquerie included, of course, the Comanche and their fellow indigenous tribes like the Oglala Sioux, Cherokee, Blackfeet and Apache among others. The perpetrators were the palefaced founders of the Empire of Liberty, an endless golden horde of settlers from the East with an iron horse and horse-soldiers whose firesticks grew more deadly with each passing year.

The Comanche became the dominant tribe of the Great Plains and presided over a huge area which included large areas of present-day Texas, Colorado, New Mexico, Oklahoma and Kansas. Comanche power depended on bison and horses, both for trading (with the Spanish and French), and raiding. They hunted the bison of the Great Plains for food and skins, and their adoption of the horse – from Spanish colonists in New Mexico – made them more mobile and thus fearsome adversaries for other native American tribes.

American bison commonly known as buffalo, were the renowned wild beasts of the Great Plains but originally had a much larger range, including much of the eastern United States and parts of Mexico. They were hunted close to extinction in the late 19th century – by the Palefaces, hence the notorious Buffalo Bill.

Both these extinction events began systematically sometime around 1865 after the paleface tribes had ended their civil war butchery which killed 640,000 and severely injured three million. It came to a grisly end 25 years later when they buried the last Indian heart and the last Buffalo cadaver at Wounded Knee in 1891.

There was no grey elephant harbinger of doom to warn America's tribal peoples, but there was however the shadow memory of the great shaggy beast that had once roamed the grassland plains in their millions. By 1890 they numbered fewer than 10,000.

It had taken just 21 years, and the infamy was complete. The transfixing of Café Josie took 21 days. (The Plains bison is no longer listed as endangered but genetically pure bison now number only about 20,000, separated into fragmented herds – which require active conservation measures).

And by mid-1989, we realised active conservation measures were required if Café Josie was to survive, especially since the lunchtime menu option had proven not to be the solution. It became abundantly clear that we needed to increase our takings substantially because one Saturday night sitting just wasn't bringing in sufficient income.

It was the one Saturday night sitting that did us in really. Once we'd started down this road, we couldn't change this practice. We should have had a sitting at 7pm and another at 9pm.

But who the hell wants to start eating an evening meal after 9pm? We might have tried that, but without any certainty of success. But our nerve failed us, and rightly or wrongly, we ruled it out.

So, if you do the maths, our income was falling woefully short of our outgoings. We needed to pull in at least 250 covers a week, given five nights of opening, Tuesday - Saturday. Do the maths – one cover approx. £20 including drinks, 250 covers = £5,000. (And there was still that lingering suspicion that we had set our pricing too low.)

Out of that £5,000 we had to pay staff, magicians and produce costs, as well the mortgage on the restaurant part of the premises. (This is not even taking into account that Rich was paying half the mortgage, representing the living accommodation, with his freelance earnings!) And then there were fixed costs like, insurance, business rates and utilities bills, gas, electricity and water.

So, it is clear, that even with a minimum 250 covers over a five-day week, things would have been tight. With actually just 50 covers on a Saturday and a desultory 80/90 more the rest of the week, Café Josie was flying on vapour, as Top Gun pilots say.

What actually kept us flying was our friendly bank manager, who believed our dream sheet projections, and cut us an open-ended overdraft facility. Our cash flow forecasts showed the sunny uplands of success with full houses on most days. Whoah!

Bourdain knew the economic score which he spelt out graphically in his opening magnum opus on the restaurant trade underbelly. He regularly cited servicing *300/400 covers a night*, more at bigger joints in the Big Apple! But, of course, *Kitchen Confidential* was only a gleam in his eye when Café Josie trundled down life's runaway and took centre-stage in the burgeoning MADchester Universe.

So, we had precious little to go on except our naive, middle-class enthusiasm and dreamscape fantasy. All would be well, we told ourselves, once we'd cast off, pulled up the anchor, made everyone fasten their seatbelts, while we gave them a night to remember. But of course, we failed to clock the grey shadow in the room as we arranged the deckchairs. And when we did, we failed to act fast enough!

Any wannabe restaurateur who wants pull off the culinary trick of creating a viable go-to diner should have no illusions about the enormous scale and complexity of the undertaking. Especially if you've tied your apron strings to providing that Holy Grail of fine dining, cooked-to-order, cordon bleu meals.

Very commendable, and precisely how we framed the eating out experience at Café Josie. However, it can't be done in the way Café Josie tried to do it. (The only way is if your eatery is a clandestine cover for something else – like gun-running, cocaine smuggling or exotic personal massage.)

As Anthony Bourdain reflected in *Kitchen Confidential*: "Operators who do well, know what they're doing from the get-go. In the face of adversity, they will redouble efforts to make the restaurant what they wanted and planned all along – hoping that the great unwashed will eventually discover it, trust it, learn to love it."

So, if you're thinking of starting a restaurant, Bourdain's advice would have been, ***don't!*** Unless you're oiling the gears with a), b), or c) above. Conjuring tricks alone don't pass muster in the big bad world of catering, with or without Colman's mustard or some other concoction like Dijonnaise.

The reason why, is the way the dining out experience divides –

Category 1*, cheap, popular fast-food, like McDonald's, Burger King, Popeye's Chicken – of universal appeal to young and old, including celebrity TV chefs! A light-hearted postscript to the Bourdain tale was provided by Jason Merder, Bourdain's road manager from 2009 to 2013, who revealed It wasn't all fine dining with the celebrity chef.*

"He was a fast-food glutton. One of the funniest things was Tony's craving for Popeye's chicken," recalled Merder. "Every time we flew through Atlanta and had an hour between flights, it

was like, 'All right, man, we're going to Popeye's.' It happened every single time, and it didn't matter what time of day it was."

Category 2 *mid-table, middle-class, special occasion eating out like Café Josie; and that includes most Asian joints, i.e. Indian and Chinese, and maybe Greek, Middle-Eastern and Turkish. The most challenging eatery to get right (i.e. profitable)*

Category 3 *top end, money-no-object, expense account dining, mostly confined to the capital (London, last time I looked) eateries fronted by chefs who know how to sweet-talk the media. (Pick any central London Italiano joint). That last is the only kind that's viable, that makes money. For the rest, go suck a pig's trotter!*

On the way to constructing your perfect eatery of course, there has to be guiding rules to keep all participants onside. The reason is there is an awful lot of moveable items around, like food raw and cooked in fridge and freezers, and gallons of drink in bottles and on tap to attract the casual gaze.

I can honestly say we needed no enforcing protocol of the kind Anthony Bourdain framed for his kitchen underbelly. And breaches of protocol were certainly not a factor in our demise. Filleted down, Bourdain's rules for any kitchen brigade can be reduced down to the Nine Bright Shiners:

1. Be Committed
2. Don't steal
3. Be on time & never call in sick
4. Never make excuses & blame others
5. Don't be lazy & sloppy

6. Be aware of human folly & assume the worst
7. Don't tell lies
8. Keep a sense of humour
9. Read good cook books

I'd always told staff that if they wanted something and if I could give it, it would happen, from a juicy steak to a bottle of wine or a bottle of beer. My mantra was 'ask, don't take'. There was only one member of staff I had to 'let go'. I had suspected theft, and then one evening, a very warm summer evening it was, he had on a large overcoat as he was about to leave the restaurant.

That was a dead giveaway that everyone could see – as in why does he need such a big coat when it's so warm? I fired him on the spot.

The next day he called in full of apologies, but I wouldn't take him back. You may think that was harsh, but everyone, including him, knew they had only to ask. It was hard for me to do this, but I had no regrets and still don't.

Returning to Bourdain's list of injunctions, *Being Committed*, is perhaps the most important. It cannot be emphasised too much that starting your own restaurant is tantamount to starting World War Z – on a microcosmic scale to be sure– and being committed certainly helps. We had much more than that – in spades. But it's not enough!

You also have to have a clear vision of reality which, despite Rovelli's prognostications, tends to be exactly what it seems.

So, you have to clear out the stardust from your eyes and take a long hard look at the actuality. It will become instantly clear that there are murmuring entities out there, zombies, grey shadows, that cannot be ignored, no matter how romantic your dream project appears.

Bourdain's injunction largely concerned the scumbags and rip-off merchants that infested the catering business all over, especially New York during his time. But what we're talking about here with this middle-class Café Josie fantasy, is making the figures add up before you get to the point of no return. Forget the romantic dream that you've just managed to get going, or you'll end up being your own worst enemy. Given the absurdly modest number of covers we were pulling from Day 1, the writing, not say elephant's shadow, was already on the wall.

The packed party bookings, many spread during the weeks in December, served to obscure what should have been clear right away. This project wasn't gonna fly even if we could have turned tables on every Saturday night.

But, of course, the magical theme bewitched us all, as well as the smug, self-satisfied patrons who must have thought they'd died and gone to heaven.

Ok, enough I think, of the love affair we had with the whole idea – we could have been running a clone of Rick's Café or a Starship Trooper flight deck complete with gremlin waiters in hideous prosthetic masks (great for the kids, as Morgan Stanley might have said) for all the difference it would have made.

So where do we go from here? Well, for a start, our foray into lunchtime opening proves the truth of the old adage, it's all about location, location, location! No, let's confine ourselves to evenings, when peeps dine out invariably for special occasions. That could work if all days were tailored for this special occasion market. A full house is a thing of beauty, is a joy forever: its loveliness increases; it will never pass into nothingness. (*pace* Keats wincing in his grave in the Protestant Cemetery, Rome).

So, for a **Category 2** eatery, how do we get there? Well, not starting out from where Café Josie did. The first thing to consider is the location could have been more central, so as to be in touch with your workaday customers from the business district of town, whose curiosity could be aroused by fulsome pictures (in the window) of magicians in action. And, of course, on your all-singing, all-dancing website!

The second thing to consider seriously, is to choose premises with twice (at least) Josie's number of covers, plus a spacious bar/lounge area with comfortable seating for at least two dozen people. You could even factor in a whole new attraction – a cocktail bar, say. You can see which way this is going, and it should already be clear that such a restaurant would be a wholly different animal to Café Josie.

Crucially, this profile would allow the eatery to be marketed big time on the special occasion, night out theme – to complement its USP of mesmerisingly civilised, table-top entertainment. (And trumpeted on your website!) Relocated and re-profiled for a minimum one full sitting (100 covers) five nights a week, there is no reason why turnover should not be stratospherically higher than Café Josie. Provided the business was marketed in a clever way. Marketing, in fact, is everything. Almost. And it could even have helped save Café Josie. Maybe!

The Yanks have a saying that it's marketing first, marketing second, marketing third. You may have the world's most brilliant product, but if no one knows about it, you're dead in the water! (Think Coca-Cola, a fizzy, sugary, soft drink everyone in the world drinks! But no one *needs* to drink Coke, even if it teaches the world to sing! Marketing, see!) Café Josie marketing budget? NIL! And even fixing the marketing would have also required an overhaul of the fundamentally dysfunctional pricing regime.

And there, Your Honour I rest my case. There's only one other key point to be made about the restaurant trade, and that concerns the premises itself, and the terms of engagement. There's no need to actually own anything, any property or shop you're going to convert. You lease it. This cuts down your initial overhead capital spend and cushions you for the initial period because you will, of course, conclude a rent holiday agreement for six months, a year, 18 months, depending on who blinks first.

So, if you allow your dream to fail this time as well, you'll only lose that initial capital your granny left you in her will, or that newspaper redundancy cash. Sobering, but relatively painless. And at least you'll have given that achingly compelling, middle-class fantasy of yours a fighting chance run-out. And all the lovely people will think the same as they did about Café Josie. It was a wonderful time to be alive, the kids loved it, the magic was transfixing customers not to leave, and the food was to die for. Whoah!

But such a scenario is looking out, back to the future. This is now, so how did Café Josie finally give up the ghost and float off back to that dreamscape in the clouds? Well, believe it or not, in the most prosaic of circumstances. The clammy fingers of big finance pulled the plug, and suddenly there was no more vapour in our engines on which to fly.

The toxic letter that arrived early in June 1989 was the real harbinger of doom. It formally announced our bank was foreclosing on our overdraft facility and demanded that we repay any outstanding debt within four weeks. If we failed, the bank would-be forced to start formal proceedings, i.e. move to a petition for bankruptcy. That would be at the end of the month, in 21 days' time.

A fire sale, as it's called in business, would have been disastrous financially, as all the assets, fixtures and fittings we'd invested in and the premises itself, would probably have been auctioned off at bargain basement prices, and only have paid off half the outstanding debts of the business. And two dreamers would probably have been made personally bankrupt, to boot.

But there was a real-life miracle on the way when the financial mafia pulled the plug. It was a man we have affectionately referred to as Gunga Din, the fakir renowned down the years for the Indian Rope Trick, thanks to that report in the *Chicago Tribune* of August 8th 1890. Travelling in India, the *Tribune* team including a photographer and a sketch artist, reported witnessing the miracle at first hand.

They saw a street fakir pull a ball of thick twine from out of a basket which he then tossed into the air. The twine unrolled until the end was high out of sight. Then a young boy, of perhaps five or six, scrambled up the erect rope and disappeared in the clouds.

But when the story appeared, the accompanying photograph showed only a sitting fakir amidst huge pile of rope on the ground. The reporter explained the discrepancy away, saying all who witnessed the trick had been hypnotised – but that didn't, of course apply to the camera, which never lies!

That didn't stop the story from creating a sensation worldwide within days, despite a retraction by the *Tribune* written by one, Fred S. Elmore. (Geddit?) The story had been essentially true but embroidered for effect – to increase the newspaper's circulation, explained its author. (Whoah! Come in Jane Austen, all is forgiven!)

And like the Loch Ness Monster, everyone even today can recount the story – without quite knowing how they came by the details. And so, the Indian Rope Trick has become an immortal part of folk memory ever since it was first described. There is no record in the *Tribune* article that the fakir's name was Gunga Din. But hey, his modern incarnation didn't let us down!

His arrival allowed us to laugh and run away, and live our life all over again another day.

13 PARADISE LOST, THE FINAL DAYS

There are only two ways to live: as if nothing is a miracle, or as if everything is. Those who attempt the absurd, achieve the impossible.

ALBERT EINSTEIN

PORTENTS OF DOOM, THE END OF THE WORLD, tend to concentrate the mind wonderfully. And so, it was with Café Josie. And we were in good company. Throughout recorded history, philosophers and poets, savants, soothsayers and clairvoyants have struggled to come to terms with an overarching vision of the End Times, that moment when darkness becomes visible and the Apocalypse subsumes everything. And life becomes hell on Earth.

Such was the universal fixation, an extraordinary popular delusion, fired continuously through the ages by the madness of crowds, and organised religion. Such mass insanity relied on belief in the existence of incorporeal beings, angels and demons, devils and witches who stalked mankind in the hours of darkness seeking to subvert innocent souls and carry off them off into eternal damnation.

From the 13th century to the dawn of the Enlightenment in the 18th, the cultural record is replete with literary and pictorial representations of this supernatural obsession – Dante, Shakespeare, Milton, Burns, have all paid accord to the legions of the damned spirits said to stalk the Earth in search of prey, the sinful, the disbeliever, the heretic.

Shakespeare's ghostly visitations are among the most compelling in the literary canon: "Tis now the very witching time of night, when churchyards yawn and Hell itself breathes forth contagion on the world". (Not unlike the Covid-19 virus from Wuhan, China, one might think).

One leading father of the Church St Gregory of Nice, regularly sermonised over the exemplar case of a nun who had failed to say grace before sitting down for her meal, and was swallowed by a demon concealed among the lettuce leaves. Whooah! If my side salads had been so contaminated, public health would have shut us down *tout de suite*!

And in art, there was Hieronymus Bosch who gave us graphic images of what awaited the carnally sinful in this vale of tears: his captured image triptych of the Garden of Earthly Delights left little to the imagination. And Dante Alighieri, in his *Divine Comedy*, waxed lyrical about the nine circles, spinning spheres that swirled round and round the soul's journey through the three realms of the dead – Hell, Purgatory and finally Heaven.

The make-up of Dante's three realms follows a common numerical pattern of 9 plus 1, for a total of 10 – that is, nine circles of the Inferno followed by Lucifer contained at its bottom; the rings of Mount Purgatory followed by the Garden of Eden crowning its summit; and nine celestial bodies of Paradiso followed by the Empyrean (the celestial dwelling place) containing the very essence of God.

In this poetic journey, the Roman poet Virgil guides the swirling Dante through Hell and Purgatory, and his ideal woman Beatrice through Heaven.

The core seven sins within Purgatory correspond to a moral scheme of love perverted, subdivided into three groups corresponding to excessive love (lust, gluttony, greed), deficient love (sloth), and malicious love (wrath envy and pride). Even Hollywood got in on this god-bothering act with director David Fincher's *Seven*, referring, of course, to those seven deadliest of Christian sins.

One sceptic chronicler Johann Weyer (1515-1588), the Dutch physician and occultist, thought that the Devil did have power to appear before people, and create illusions. But these were the handiwork of magicians not witches, whose persecution he fulminated against in his tract, *De Praestigiis Daemonum* (On illusions of Demons).

He even provided, for the first time, a precise calculation of the number of these spirit demons – 7,450,926 in total, divided into 26 battalions, each commanded by a captain.

Given such outer-galactic odds, what hope did Mankind have for redemption in this cosmic battle against the massed legions of Beelzebub, the satanic Prince of all Evil? Not much Lord Copper, as Oscar Wilde might have said.

And that was not all. In the freewheeling, eschatologically fevered ramblings of John Milton's epic blank verse poem *Paradise Lost*, legions of angelic denominations were cast out from a mythical construct called Heaven, as Adam and Eve were expelled from another mythical creation the Garden of Eden – on the orders of another suitably mystical and mysterious construct called God.

These turncoat angels (as in ganging up with Satan over on the dark side) were home-based in another mythical construct called Hell. Whether they were sent to wrong address scholars were still debating, when Enlightenment thinking finally broke through in the 18th century.

Reginald Scot's book *The Discoverie of Witchcraft* certainly helped spark this shift in thinking. As did increasing fossil evidence that challenged Armagh Archbishop James Ussher's calculation that the world was created at around 4pm on the afternoon of 23rd October, in 4004 BC.

It was to counteract such mass delusions that *Discoverie,* the first book on conjuring and the magical arts was written 500 years ago by Reginald Scot. It was published in 1584 around the same time as the treatise, *Daemonolgie* written by no lesser person than King James VI Scotland (later James I of England). The "wisest fool in Christendom" succeeded to the English throne on the death of Elizabeth I in 1603. He immediately ordered all copies of *Discoverie* to be burned. There soon followed an orgy of witch-hunting.

So, the nation's God-given ruler (Divine Right 'n' all) was complicit in the madness that led to an orgy of judicial killing across Europe over two centuries between 1550 and 1750. Witchcraft was blamed for very human sorrow, from ill-health to child mortality in childbirth, from bad harvests to bad weather.

In his meticulously documented account, Scot demolishes the mass delusion of belief in supernatural powers. (He was a magistrate as well as philosopher and had attended witch trials, helping many women to be acquitted). He shows all examples of witchcraft cited by learned figures were nothing more than clever sleight-of-hand by conjurors, tricks by masters of the dark arts of deception. Sounds like a dead ringer for any Café Josie magician!

But across England and much of the Continent such beliefs persisted. (Especially in Germany, where witch-hunting was driven by the notorious Jacob Sprenger and his "hammer of witches" diatribe *Malleus Maleficarum*, leading to the execution of maybe 800 witches every year in many cities*)*. In England alone during the 17th century, the mass persecution of so-called witches saw at least 40,000 horrifically put to death, according to court records.

And no wonder – more shockingly, witches were said to be transported to and from their nefarious work on the back of the Devil himself! And when they were dropped off by this celestial taxi, they found ingress into any luckless person's house by whispering themselves into nothing more than an unearthly ball of vapour and slipping through dwelling's keyhole. (A bit like how

Conan Doyle thought Houdini carried out his more baffling feats of escapology).

Records are notoriously difficult to pin down, but across Europe, it is estimated at least 350,000 supposed witches were slaughtered, burned, hanged or otherwise executed on the orders of special tribunals set up to hunt them down (1550-1750). All of which turned on the madness of crowds. And it was to address this overarching insanity that Scot wrote his groundbreaking volume, *Discoverie,* the first conjuror's manual, and for which we should all be grateful.

But nothing comes close to a real hell on Earth than the man-made inferno of the titanic, all-tank battle at Kursk in July 1943. No fewer than 10,000 of these iron-clad monsters of war were involved, and the outcome was the end of Operation Barbarossa, and death knell of Adolf Hitler's ambition for world domination. Kursk was absolutely a real-life episode that came as close to hell on earth as any of the metaphysical nightmares dreamt up by the legion of god-botherers who held civilisation in their sway for 2,000 years.

Kursk was for real. Just as real as the situation in which we at Café Josie found ourselves in June 1989, as the MADchester decade played itself out. True, there were no Tiger panzers involved, but we were looking down the barrel of a bankruptcy Bofors gun, and there didn't seem any way out.

So, there's no cash to spare, or any sloshing around in our bank account that had been frozen. We had to survive until the end of July, and somehow pay wages and producers, and we were still open for business. Not exactly the best position to be in. What do we do? We can't just shut up shop. We've got to somehow trade our way through the next four weeks, and then shut up shop, closing early for the summer, we could announce. But not without some cash leeway.

Rich said he'd pile in a grand from his personal account, but first we had to put the business up for sale, so that we didn't crash out and succumb to that Bofors bankruptcy gun. The business estate agents were around in 24 hours, and valued Café Josie at £140,000. We got that figure confirmed in writing, and physically took it over to the bank.

In return, we got some breathing space, the bank agreeing to pay June staff wages, and current turnover produce costs, which were painfully low. All other liabilities were to be negotiated and arranged on sale of the business, said the bank. Phew!

So now we had to wrap up the whole project as smoothly and discreetly as we could, to avoid any embarrassing explanations. All within 21 days!

We told only key staff members, including our main man chef Kim and chief waiter-on Hedda. Kim said he was really sorry, but that he'd like to move on right away, in fact at the end of the month. Hedda, said she'd stay. But we kept calm and carried on because that's what we always did.

So, when Kim moved on to pastures new at the end of June, I took over as head chef and Donna moved up to second chef. Donna was a catering student when she joined us, and under my wing she blossomed and so was more than capable of stepping up to the plate. She alone knew that when we closed at the end of July, we would not be reopening in September.

Three days into that first week in June, the business agents told us a sale could be arranged and completed within four to six weeks, and there had already been a few enquiries. The Bofors gun menace was receding, slightly. We reckoned a sale at £140,000 would pay off all our debts and liabilities, but with little to spare, and leaving us homeless. Apocalypse was now looming.

That's when Gunga Din (minus Indian Rope Trick) stepped into the picture. Or more precisely came to dinner. The family who had booked a table for four were headed by a decidedly Asian father, who had booked the table during the week we had put the premises up for sale. He gave his name as Ashwan el-Edin for the bookings diary and said he would be accompanied by his wife (in colourful sari), and two young daughters.

We didn't think there was anything special about the booking and didn't really pay much attention to them – except of course, when the girls were asked if they'd like to see some magic. Which was answered with a rousing, "Oh, yes please!", and cheers of excited laughter.

I think Rich went over and did the chop cup with sponge balls, but no spider! And he finished with the Invisible Deck for Mrs el-Edin, to a round applause from her husband.

That Saturday we had been three-quarters full – it was mid-summer – and we were already getting withdrawal pains about what lay ahead. I think the guest magician was David Jones, who'd been with us from the earliest days.

I recall Rich telling me he'd joined us on the recommendation of Rovi, and he never let us down. Nor did he that evening. He toured the tables with his signature coin chicanery and impossible mental card revelations, among other mysteries. Great stuff!

Dave said he had fond memories of Café Josie and the staff. And especially the head Maîtresse D' Hedda. And he'll never forget the night a seven-year-old girl, saw through his coin matrix routine! Or the time a diner became convinced he had genuine psychic powers!

"I have great memories of working at the Café – it was the first venue that gave me the opportunity of performing regularly for 'real' people and to hone my act," recalled Dave. "And although I was a happily married man at the time, I fell a bit in love with Hedda, the beautiful front-of-house person.

"I got on with head barman, Eddie (Fast Eddie) Sherwood, very well. I was (and still am) a big fan of The Bard of Salford – punk poet, John Cooper Clarke. I mentioned this to Eddie, and he told me he used to share a flat with him.

"He said that they would arrange to meet up in a pub, and John didn't turn up until five minutes before closing time – it had taken him an hour and a half to coax his hair into that distinctive haystack style! Eddie told me that John had written a poem about him, and I asked which one. 'Twat' he said!

"Blimey - why did he write that Eddie?" "I dunno – I think it might have been because I slept with his girlfriend!" I met John a few years later and mentioned Eddie to him. John was very complimentary – 'Eddie Sherwood – great bloke' he said! Obviously, he had been forgiven.

"I also remember Kim – the 'Rave' loving head Chef. One of the 'perks' of working at Café Josie was a free meal at the end of the night – I remember being introduced to the exotic (at the time) Chicken Szechuan, one of Josie's specialties. He would make us all –

magicians and staff – a batch and then head off to the Hacienda till the small hours.

"The customers were a varied lot too – gangsters, businessmen, husbands and wives, and even children. You know what they say about working with kids! In the restaurant, I used to perform a clever sleight-of-hand trick with cards and coins, generally known among magicians as *Matrix*. It is one of those tricks where the method is so clever, you can't help but smile in admiration for the inventor each time you do it.

"It fools everyone who sees it! Except …. a little seven-year-old girl who watched me perform it one night, and then immediately proceeded to accurately dissect every step of the method, and even had a go at doing it herself! You could meet all sorts in Café Josie! I was entertaining a couple one evening and the wife was utterly convinced I had 'genuine' magic powers, even though the tricks I was doing were about as far removed from 'Black Magic' as you could possibly get. I just could not convince her that it was sleight-of-hand! She quizzed me for ages about where I had obtained my 'psychic' gifts.

"I was a fan of the Irish Rock band Thin Lizzy. The lead singer was Phil Lynott, whose mum owned a hotel not far from Café Josie. One day, a small dumpy little man came in with some friends, and I performed at his table. We got talking, and he said: "Phil Lynott wrote a song about me – they call me 'Jimmy the Weed'!

"I immediately realized I was talking to the subject on one of my favourite Thin Lizzy tracks – 'Johnny the Fox meets Jimmy the Weed'! The track is a song about the sinister world of crime, although Jimmy himself was a very charming man.

"My day job at the time was working for Duerr's Jams in Old Trafford. I eventually started to earn more by performing magic at Café Josie than in my day job, and I regard my time at the restaurant as the springboard for me turning full time pro as a magician a few years later. So, it's true to say the Café Josie really did change my life!"

For Dave, that Saturday had been just another successful night of legerdemain. Just like the diners, he knew nothing of the impending storm that was about to engulf us. And so, a good time was had by all, before our customers gradually took their leave of Café Josie at the end of service. All except the Indian family. Mr Ashwan el-Edin, waited until the place was completely empty and then asked Rich whether he could have a quiet word with the two of us.

I joined Rich and Mr el-Edin came straight to the point. He said he and his family had enjoyed the meal and the magic, and he was interested in buying the place. Could he have a look at the kitchen and the living accommodation? I said no problem and showed them around everywhere.

When the tour was over, Mr el-Edin was all smiles. "Wonderful," he said. "You have a wonderful place here. I've been in touch with your agents, they say the premises are still on the market. So, you've not made a sale yet? "

We confirmed we had still not agreed a sale, and asked if he was thinking of making an offer? He nodded and asked what sort of figure had we in mind? We had to think fast. Obviously, he knew the agents' asking price of £140,000 but we were looking for a higher figure to give us some flexibility when we vacated premises homeless. That's when Rich came straight out and said £165,000!

Without batting an eyelid or any further ado, Mr el-Edin said "Done!" And that was it. We all shook hands and he said he'd be in touch with our agents. He said he was looking for the earliest possible exchange of contracts. We said so were we and bade each other goodnight. We had a done deal, on the most favourable terms. So Gunga Din had weaved his magic spell, rope trick or no.

It was unbelievable. We were out with a solid cushion of at least £25,000 to help us on our way. Now we had to count down the days to an exchange of contract, days during which we would be servicing our last diners, while we searched for a new family home. Café Josie had just weeks left to live, and we all prepared for the end to an amazing journey.

The key date that lay immediately ahead was my parents' 40th wedding anniversary on 18th June, a Sunday which was also Father's Day. I had been planning to put on the biggest celebration they'd ever seen, right from the opening of Café Josie. Now the party was going to be a farewell swan song – with some sleight-of-hand which kept it from my Mum.

I had to make up names in the bookings diary to ensure Mum didn't book anyone in if she answered the phone. And I have to say, as the day came closer, she did, at one point, remark we were fully booked on the night before their anniversary. I just don't know what she must have thought. Everything was so top secret.

I'd invited relatives to come down from Scotland, and others from Birmingham and Greater Manchester, and told them to bring their friends. But we told them to keep it all hush-hush. Lee, one of our waiters made a cake, it was a couch with my parents' then grandchildren, Martyn, James, Michael and Danielle sitting on it – it was brilliant! And I had another cake made with red roses, as well.

Then the anniversary party weekend came round, and I seemed as busy as ever in the restaurant. Mum remarked that it was a pity we couldn't celebrate with a dinner at Café Josie – because the bookings diary had been fully booked for weeks! (LOL).

That's what she told my sister Janet and husband Tony when they picked up Mum and Dad in the early evening. And even when they arrived at the Café to be greeted by me in an evening dress, it still hadn't clicked. Not until Mum suddenly saw her sister from Scotland – and then they suddenly both realised it was all for them! Mum was shaking as I pressed a drink into her hand.

It was a wonderful evening. Danielle wore a pretty dress, a red bodice with black lace skirt specially bought for the occasion. Many of those friends and relatives are no longer with us, including my Dad. But I have the memories and the photos from that night, which I'll always treasure.

The last event that Café Josie hosted was Danielle's 4th birthday party. We had games, magicians, party food and fun. That was the last night those premises would hear the shrieks of wonder and delight which had delighted so many people over those two crazy years of the MADchester Universe. Two glorious years when we had blazed a starry trail across the cultural zeitgeist of Greater Manchester.

And now the dream had died, and I thought I would be grateful for the rest after working sometimes 18 hours a day, which had taken its toll. I remember a customer once remarking how wonderful it must be to only open in the evenings and have the day to myself! Of such stuff are all our dreams made! I just nodded and smiled.

Anthony Bourdain's farewell words:
"The most dangerous species of restaurant owner is the the one who gets into the business for love. Love for the song styling of Gershwin, love for the regional cuisine of rural Mexico, love of 18th century French antiques, love of that great Bogie film.

"Writing anything is a treason of sorts. Even the cold recitation of facts is never the thing in itself. Who knows what events in this long-ago past inspire this rare display of emotion. And who needs to know? I just know what I've seen. And I understand. It makes perfect sense. What I set out to do was write a book that my fellow cooks and restaurant lifers would find entertaining and true."

Leonard Cohen wrote in song:
Dance me through the panic, till I'm gathered safely in:
 Oh, let me see your beauty when the witnesses are gone;
Let me feel you moving like they do in Babylon;
Show me slowly, what I only know the limits of;
Dance me to the end of love . . .

July came round, and now with the Café closing in on darkness awaiting its new guardians on the exchange of a contract, our task was to find a new home and quickly so that we didn't end up being bundled out of Barlow Moor Road unceremoniously. At least, I'd managed to get a school place for Danielle from January and had taken her out of nursery.

Sooner than expected, we chanced upon our new abode and had taken possession still with a few weeks to spare in late July, so we could take our time packing. Then suddenly, it was all over. The day before we left, I deep-cleaned the kitchen at Café Josie one last time. Why, I don't know.

Then we were gone . . . To pastures new, swirling towards Dante Alighieri's Ninth Circle of Hell, Treachery. But that's another story . . .

Boxing clever... Danielle aged 4 dons her Dad's gloves

PASTSCRIPT: BACK TO THE FUTURE

*All the world's a stage and all the
men and women merely players.*

SHAKESPEARE, *AS YOU LIKE IT*, ACT II, SCENE VII

QUANTUM PHYSICISTS HAVE LONG BEEN – as in nano-light seconds – been wrestling with the elusive theoretical concept of spatial lensing, or stretching time. And Hollywood has long – ditto – had the field to itself, dabbling in some of the most absurdly wild flights of fancy ever proposed in an elevator pitch for time travel. At its worst, it was stuff like those several, fevered disquisitions on H.G.Wells' *Time Machine*. But there's been a lot of other time traveller junk in there, too. Until now.

The question has been always been, doesn't such telescoping of the space-time continuum compress conscious memories out of existence, so that the traveller stepping into a new time frame is unaware he's made such a prodigious leap? How can such a traveller know it all – times past and present? (The future can only be idle speculation).

How can such a traveller know the mind of God, as Einstein asked. That's the Hollywood script that's yet to be written. Although Tinseltown's groundbreaking tale *Source Code*, 2011, directed by Duncan Jones (David Bowie's son), went close with the time traveller who knows nothing!

But that was a one-off and failed to address the precise time-travel mechanism. So, while we're still waiting, I'll hand over to Danielle, whose concertina scrambling of space-time recollections are herewith unpicked . . .

Danielle Karameneh Adamson (aged four at the time) and now in her thirties, remembers:

Strange, what desire will make foolish people do.
WICKED GAME

Once upon a time, at the very centrepoint of the universe, there was a magic castle with secrets, a castle alive with explosions of beauty, neon lights of mystery and wonderment dancing on the tip of every tongue. Its walls were laced with rose petal threading, cloaked in the shadows cast by the rest of the galaxy, adding to its elemental appeal.

Now there's a catch, of course. There's always a catch, and in this case, it was perspective. The castle had a name, well-known, I've come to hear, and was alive with wonders untold. But as Cinderella herself came to realise, the ticking clock is never kind. And so, the castle only came alive for a few hours at a time, and then only ever at night.

So, the castle was an alluring vampire, a rush of awe, a drug of choice, a stand-out fixation, so far outta the box that to any transient outsider, the mirage appeared an unreal cordon bleu buffet, a billion-dollar banquet show, a total f**king head trip in the middle of Manchester.

Only The Hive could have dreamt up something like this, something like Café Josie. And this is the fleeting, obscurantist memoir of someone on the inside, deep undercover, behind the scenes. So deep in fact, that the import of this extract is quite obviously totally compromised, as we shall see.

And yet, and yet . . . despite that fact that the deepest memories I've dug out of the vault can both annoy and amuse, I pray you, give me some space as I bite. Because it's all here, wrapped in a warming, soothing, energy rush to the senses that will fill the nostrils to overflowing. Aromas of delight and taste dissolved into a galactic supernova of beating, bleeding heart madness, harnessed, bottled, and distilled to perfection. Mum, it was like Willie Wonka on speed, only better.

And at the castle gates, Mistress Josie's waved enchantments enveloped the visitor's whole being with disarming ease. All wands, muggle and wizard alike, were surrendered without question upon their owners being granted entry. For they were being admitted to the most unique experience one could have in the City of Bees at nightfall, here at the dark, rusting epicentre of what was once a city's industrial glory.

And it wasn't just for the show that these pilgrims searching for the citadel of the dark arts came. No, they knew instinctively there was more, much more. And we're about to get into that, don't worry. I know that's what you really lined up for, too. My words can be distracting, but that's the nature of misdirection. And a riddler never leaves you satisfied you know . . . No, they came to taste the MADchester universe, to partake of the elemental magic that was Josie's Café Josie.

My father had no illusions about this. He always said, and still does to this day, that the "real magic happens in the kitchen". Now that's a sentiment I can tip my hat to. An absolute truth, the only absolute I can ever be sure of when it comes to him. I couldn't agree more.

It was a castle of perplexing delights where everything begged an answer. As in, the how, the why, the where, and the when, and what the f**k just happened? With every turn, there was a new conundrum.

But one thing was certain, that the delicious fare Josie served up from the fires of backstage chaos was the most magical thing about the place, and a superb gastronomic reality nobody ever doubted.

Most magic, I believe, begins with good intentions. (When you create a universe, its natural, inevitable purpose is to become a gift, as The Creator would surely say to our man Neo). I have often looked upon homo sapiens with disgust at our species' ineffable ability to transform a gift into a curse.

But ultimately, we can't make a leopard change its spots. And sometimes even a cursed thing has the potential to be transformed into a thing of beauty, a joy forever. Amen. Cue astoundingly white light glitterings.

Silly Rabbit! Tricks are for Kids!

Back in the day, I lived in a world of my own, a gifted world of fantastical turns, twists, and tricks. But it was the trips, glorious trips on my tricycle that stand out in my childhood dreams.

Like a PG version of *The Shining*, there I was tiny little me on my tricycle speeding around the restaurant floor, under tables, through tablecloths, screeching around the pink padded chairs as my aunt and granny tried desperately to ready the place in my wake.

It was a happy-go-lucky, wicked game to play – how many grannies does it take to reset a room of fancy tables with a little rabbit whizzing circles around her…? The age-old question of what's at the end of the rainbow never troubled me. I knew where it ended and began! And no Magician's Code secrets will be unlocked (magicians secrets are sacred). So, no need for any apology here, Dad, when I reveal the simple truth – magic begins in a locked trunk, and ends in a giant wardrobe that could rival Narnia.

Now you must understand, if you tell a child that something is not a toy, that child will learn to unpick a lock, and indeed your pockets, pretty damn quickly. And if you are a wizard, this can be problematic. I can only assume my father also learned quickly from me, and remembered to pack at least two spares of everything wherever he went … Lumos Maxima.

Leonard Cohen wrote:
Show me slowly, what I only know the limits of,
Dance me to the end of love …

APPENDIX: SECRETS FOR SALE

Ace Richard SandersFX
Astral Projection Sankey Magic
Blank Magic of Craig Petty World Magic Shop
Bullet Party John Bannon BigBlindMedia
Bullet Proof Magic Sankey Magic
Cataclysm Alakazam Magic UK
Cheek to Cheek Oz Pearlman Penguin Magic
Collateral Ring & String Diamond Jim Tyler
Fiber Optics Extended (richard)sandersfx.com
Extractor E2 Alakazam Magic UK
Fuze T&R WizardFX World Magic Shop
Grand Opening Sankey Magic
Heinstein's Dream T&R card Karl Hein
Hundred Dollar Miracles Sankey Magic
Imagine SMProductionz.com
Inferno Joshua Jay Vanishing Inc. & CardShark
Invisible Sankey Magic
Last Laugh Mark Elsdon Alakazam Magic UK
Loops Guerrilla Guide Daniel Garcia
M-Case Mickael Chatelain
Mind-Bending Sankey Magic
Mix 'n' Mingle Shaun McCree Alakazam Magic UK
Move Zero 1, 2, & 3 John Bannon BigBlindMedia
Ninja+ Ring Link Matthew Garrett
One Twist T&R Axel Hecklau
Parlour Live & Explained C. Petty World Magic Shop
Revolutionary Card Magic Sankey Magic
Ring Flight Revolution PropDog
Simplimental Mark Elsdon Full52 Productions

Spontaneous Combustion Sankey Magic
Stand & Deliver! Shaun McCree Alakazam Magic UK
Touched Morgen Strebler SansMinds
Twisted Sisters John Bannon Murphy's Magic
Unicorn Coin in Bottle Nicholas Einhorn

ABOUT THE AUTHORS

Josephine Adamson (nee Gannon) was educated at Manchester Central Grammar School for Girls and went on to work as an advertising administrator at a number of leading Manchester agencies including Rowlinson Broughton (razor-sharp creatives) and JWT (bunch of neo-nazi/bungling nancy boys). In the mid-1970s she hitched a ride aboard *New Manchester Review* a new publication set up by a group of Manchester University alumni including husband-to-be Richard. *New Manchester Review* claimed to be the Cottonopolis version of *Time Out* and *Private Eye* but failed to outlive the darkness of the Thatcherite night. Josie bided her time before being consumed by the insanity of becoming a restaurateur. After Café Josie's vanishing act, Josie became a personal therapist, before retiring to write this memoir, at the urging of the Café's masters of the dark arts whose legerdemain had given the restaurant such a unique character.

Richard Adamson was a Fleet Street journalist for more than 25 years serving time with, among others, the *Daily Telegraph*, *Daily Express*, *Daily Mail*, *Guardian*, and *Daily Mirror*, before escaping into Academe at the Universities of Westminster and Buckingham. It was an article for the Sunday Mirror magazine in 1995 that spawned *Bogota Bandit*, his El Dorado biography of Man United's penalty king. His publishers Mainstream were still vainly awaiting his promised follow-up book on the American civil war's ghost ship when they were taken over in 2005 by Penguin Random House. In 2018, he was diagnosed with MS and has since been receiving treatment at a specialist clinic in Austria. Therapists advise they might not be able to bend the laws of nature. But, he says, the audience shouldn't blink, or they'll miss his greatest vanishing act.

Printed in Great Britain
by Amazon